Aaron Smith is a dear friend of the Cofer family and a gifted leader in the UPPERROOM community. *BIG JESUS* carries a childlike faith in the character and nature of Jesus in our everyday life. If you know Aaron and his wife Sarahbeth, you know they carry an expectation of Jesus revealing Himself in all parts of life. The stories and truths shared in this book will inspire you to get rid of any box you have put Jesus in based on limited thinking or unbelief. Does Jesus want to reveal Himself in the details, mistakes, you name it, of our lives? Absolutely, and *BIG JESUS* will lead you to greater faith in the God who wants to break every box we try to put Him in. Enjoy this faith-filled book with true stories of Jesus revealing just how big He is.

—**CHASE AND LINDY COFER,** Circuit Riders

BIG JESUS captures the reality a generation needs right now—nothing can eclipse Jesus, ever! The longing to see victory, breakthrough, and purpose in life is at an all-time high, and *BIG JESUS* will help reframe all of this and more. Aaron has risen as a strong voice to champion this message, and I'm excited to see this work navigate you into a place of presence and strength. Enjoy!

—**CHRIS ESTRADA,** Missions Me

Aaron Smith is by far the wildest man of faith, who is grounded in what God is doing locally but has never lost vision of what God's doing globally! I believe this book, *BIG JESUS*, will help you look at your life ahead with faith and courage, with great expectation of what Jesus can do!

—**BRIAN BARCELONA,** One Voice Student Ministries

For too long, well-meaning believers have reduced Jesus to the confines of their limited life experience and imagination. We have placed Him in a box that our finite minds can comprehend. In *BIG JESUS*, Aaron Smith illustrates the magnitude of what Jesus is ready and able to do. He shatters the box of unbelief by sharing story after story of Jesus' miraculous faithfulness in his life. Aaron is one of this generation's greatest young leaders. He is filled with a conviction that Jesus cannot and will not be confined, and he is setting young people free with that same revelation.

—**LYLE PHILLIPS,** Legacy Nashville Church

Now, more than ever, we need a generation that believes JESUS is BIG. In his book, Aaron Smith portrays Jesus as bigger than any circumstance, issue, or crisis happening on the earth. *BIG JESUS* imparts faith to its readers and opens the eyes of your heart to see boxes that we sometimes put JESUS in! I deeply love Aaron and have watched him become consumed with a lifestyle of prayer and hunger for God's word. I believe the Lord is using his passion for God like a flame to catch young believers' hearts on fire!

—**COREY RUSSELL,** Corey Russell Online

I believe the message of *BIG JESUS* is long overdue. It's time for believers to let Jesus out of their boxes and see Him for who He really is. In this book, Aaron tells of faith-filled experiences that will offend our religious ideologies and portray just how big our God really is! It's time for the world to see a big Jesus.

—**ELYSSA SMITH,** UPPERROOM

BIG JESUS is a faith building, encounter-based book. For too long, believers have kept Jesus in a box of religion that seeks to comprehend Him with our earthly minds. This simply cannot be. He cannot be contained, and as you read this book, you will see through Aaron's daily life testimonies that Jesus does not want to be confined to what we think He can do but wants to blow our minds with just how vast and incomprehensible He really is. I challenge you to ask Jesus to tear down any wall of religion you may have as you read. If you let it, this book will help you encounter a man named Jesus that's behind the pages, the word made flesh is waiting to speak to you and show you how big He is and how much He loves you.

—SARAHBETH SMITH, UPPERROOM

God wants to give Himself to us without limits. It's us who end up putting the limits on God. These limits might seem small and unnoticed, but they grow. They eventually make us overly skeptical and avoid the spaces and places God wants to show up in miraculous ways. We suffer when Jesus is boxed in and we need someone to get us out. *BIG JESUS* is a right word in a right season with stories that will inspire you and bring you to tears. Aaron's on a mission to destroy those limits and draw us into the awe that comes from seeing Jesus rightly. *BIG JESUS* pushes with just the right amount of healthy pressure to get you to give up limiting beliefs about Jesus and yourself. Aaron is pulling a generation to an anchor stronger than the tide of popular culture. He is on a quest to see a generation dare to believe Jesus truly is bigger..

—CHRIS CRUZ, Bethel Church

BIG JESUS is a brilliant challenge to smash the man-made boxes and limiting beliefs we each cling to, and embrace a wholehearted, wild life with God, one that goes beyond what we could ever imagine. Aaron's call to evaluate your own self-imposed constructs and ideas of Jesus will inevitably lead you into a fuller and more fulfilling experience in your own relationship with God. This book reminds us all that life with God is a grand adventure, one that's meant to be embraced on God's terms, not ours. It's infinitely better that way!

—**DANIEL MADDRY,** Youth Pastor Co

"Jesus is the sole remedy for every issue in every single life – past, present, and future. The Son of God is the Father's obsession and His only sermon to mankind. I thank the Holy Spirit for stirring this next generation to exalt the name of Jesus and make this life all about Him. Simplicity is piercing to the human heart, and I'm thankful for Aaron's life. May the Lord raise up a company like Aaron, who will unapologetically declare Heaven's Song….Jesus Christ, Son of the Living God."

—**MICHAEL KOULIANOS,** Jesus Image

In the same way that a telescope magnifies the stars, the very best kind of Bible teaching magnifies Jesus. It doesn't make Him bigger - that would be impossible - but, just like that telescope, it focuses us in, helping us realize that our Subject is even more awesome than we had imagined. Aaron's wonderful book is a brilliant magnifier. On every single page, through scripture and personal stories, he amplifies the glory and grace of Christ, encouraging us into a life of faith and adventure. No one needs a small god. This inspiring book gives us a timely and vital reminder that we worship a BIG JESUS.

—**MATT AND BETH REDMAN,** Singer/Songwriter

Aaron Smith is a gentle giant. His tender heart towards God and man is evident in the language in this book that you now hold in your hand, *BIG JESUS*. Aaron's personal discovery of the "bigness" of God in his own life story is beautiful and transparent. I believe his authentic humility has caused tremors in the dark world every time he takes a step of faith. He's not big in stature, but there is a weightiness to each step and a confidence supporting every word. May you discover for yourself a BIG JESUS!!!

—**DAVID BINION,** Dwell Church

How easy it can be to neuter the nature of Jesus, water down His wonder and quiet the call He extended without even realizing it. When we do, we run the risk of missing Him and missing our purpose in Him. In *BIG JESUS*, Aaron Smith magnifies Jesus and amplifies His call all over again, inviting the reader to cut loose the boxes we've placed Him in. Aaron invites a generation that knows they are called to something great, to know Jesus in His greatness all over again through his authentic life example of surrender and passion.

—**KALLEY HEILIGENTHAL,** Singer/Songwriter

STORIES OF FAITH THAT EXPOSE THE BOXES WE PUT HIM IN

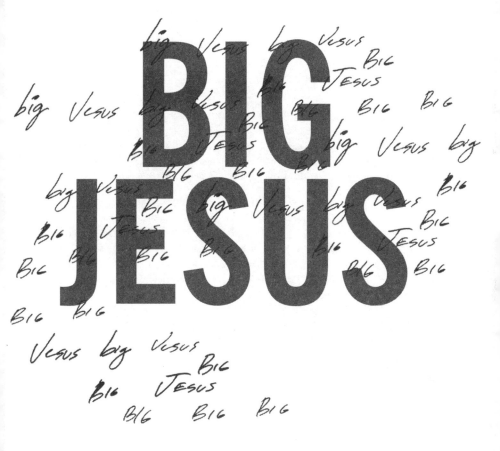

BIG JESUS

aaron w. smith

Edited by Chelsea Slade
Cover Design and art by Neww Creative, Inc.

UPRM

Published by UPPERROOM Global, Inc.
Publisher Website: upperroom.co

Paperback ISBN: 9781952421334
Hardcover ISBN: 9781952421334
eISBN: 9781952421334
Library of Congress Control Number: 2023903994

First Edition
Printed in the United States

DEDICATION

Holy Spirit,
Without you, I would still have God in a box. Thank you for
your voice and your leadership.

Jesus,
The works of your hands are meant to be remembered. May
these pages, chapters, and stories be a memorial stone to you.

Rosie and Shepard,
I hope your mother and I live in such a way that forever paints the
picture to you that there is nothing in our lives as big as Jesus.

Beautiful Sarahbeth,
I love you deeply. Words fall short of all that you mean to me.

CONTENTS

FOREWORD

I have known Aaron Smith for more than a decade. When we first met, he was 19 years old, a Bible school student with a fairly defined plan for his future. He was driven, gifted, and ready to take on life as a young leader. That was until he met me. I am not certain if he would describe it this way, but I recall Aaron had a bit of hesitancy about the UPPERROOM when he first came to our community. It wasn't necessarily *what* we were doing, but *how* we were doing it.

From the onset of our friendship, Aaron had a lot of questions about leadership. These questions were coming from a true desire and calling to lead God's people. Afterall, he was in Bible school and training to be in full time ministry. It was apparent to him and everyone that knew Aaron, that he was called to lead for Jesus. He is a natural born leader. Yet, Jesus had a different plan for Aaron. He took Aaron and his dreams, gifts, and plans, and buried them in the "soil" of our community. Jesus planted this young, gifted visionary in the dark soil of community and ministry within our church. Over time, he developed a relationship with me and my family. He would come to the house and ask A LOT of questions. He wanted to understand our approach to church leadership, pastoring, and the culture. He submitted to what He did not understand and trusted the process of maturing as a leader.

Since that time, I have had the opportunity to watch Aaron grow up. He has been employed at the UPPERROOM as a pastor for the last 10 years. He met his wife, I officiated his wedding, he became a father of two, and I have had the privilege of leading a weekly prayer set with him. I have had a front row seat to Aaron's spiritual development and maturity as a leader. I have watched God form and shape His leadership in Aaron's life. I have been so impressed with Aaron's submission to Jesus's leadership and work in his life.

It is important for you to know my history with Aaron to understand the words in this book. You see, for some time I have sensed that God is raising up a new breed of young leaders like Aaron Smith. These leaders will be some of the most anointed, influential leaders the earth has known. The defining difference in their leadership won't be their abilities, gifts, or charisma. The defining mark of their leadership will be God's leadership through them. It will be a private life and history of intimacy with God that will lead them to their positions of influence and authority. Their leadership will be the fruit of God's unique leadership and their ability to humbly follow Him. It will resemble the early leaders of the church. These early leaders were those who deserted and denied Him and anyone who would follow the disciples would know about their history with Jesus. These guys were not quali-fied in the "natural" to be the leaders that they would eventually become. Yet, it was Jesus's leadership through them that marked them as leaders. In Acts 4:13 (NLT) the religious leaders "*could see that Peter and John were ordinary men with no special training in the Scriptures. They also recognized them as men who had been with Jesus.*"

Jesus was really the only thing Peter and John had going for them.

The same can be said about the leaders emerging today. Be-yond giftings, personalities, and charisma, leadership in the fu-ture is going to be marked by God's leadership alone. These fol-lowers of Jesus will be leaders for Jesus because of their unique ability to first follow Him. This may seem like a small thing at face value, but it will be the defining mark for the days ahead. This delineation in future leaders will become evident as we see them arise and steward greater influence and authority. Aaron Smith is one of these leaders. Is he gifted? Extremely. Is he a leader? For sure. Is he wise and articulate? Beyond most. Heck, he has a beautiful wife and family and can shoot a three pointer like few I know.

Yet, none of that is what makes Aaron the person and leader that he is today. The distinguishing mark of Aaron's life is his commitment to follow Jesus's leadership in everything. Aaron Smith has submitted to and learned the ways of Jesus's leadership.

The testimonies in BIG JESUS are just the beginning of a young man's pursuit of Jesus. This pursuit has been marked by the supernatural leadership of Jesus Himself. The stories will ignite your hunger and passion for Jesus. Most importantly, they will ignite your faith. In the days ahead, we must have a knowledge of a *BIG JESUS*. The supernatural will become more and more natural in the church again. It will be the fruit of leaders that get out of the way to let the leadership of Jesus take stage. Thank you, Aaron, for writing this book. Thank you, Aaron, for following and knowing a Jesus who is bigger than we realize and able to do immeasurably more than we can imagine. - You are a remarkable leader because you are a remarkable follower. - Your life is admirable and your love for Jesus is contagious.

—MICHAEL MILLER, UPPERROOM

BIG JESUS

We need a BIG Jesus.
A Jesus that's Bigger than we can imagine. Larger than we can fathom. And grander than we can think up.

We need a BIG Jesus.
A Jesus that destroys our paradigms. Exposes our boxes. And shatters every form of dead religion.

We need a BIG Jesus.
A Jesus that's not just a little higher than the heavens, but He is completely outside the hierarchy of life.

We need a BIG Jesus.
A Jesus that's louder than the noise of fear. Stronger than culture's agenda. Greater than the voice of raging kings.

We need a BIG Jesus.
A Jesus that rips away shame's hold. Stomps on death's sting. Punches sin back to the grave.

We need a BIG Jesus.
A Jesus that outshines every voice that speaks for Him, saves every hand that reaches to Him. And captivates every eye that looks at Him.

We need a BIG Jesus.

See this is *the JESUS* that whispered, "peace be still," and the waves obeyed. This is *the JESUS* that snatched Lazarus back from the grave. This is *the JESUS* who is God wrapped in flesh and the only one who can save.

HE is a **BIG JESUS.**

This is *the JESUS* that closed the mouths of lions, showed up in flames of fire, and told Hades, "Those keys are mine."

HE is a **BIG JESUS.**

This is *the JESUS* that called the dead to rise, took the world by surprise, and reconciled every life back to Him.

HE is a **BIG JESUS.**

This is *the JESUS* that was whipped for every sin. That was pierced for all men. And TRULY is coming back again.

We need this **BIG JESUS.**

Who is and forever will be **OUR KING**.

PROLOGUE

Hi. Welcome to BIG JESUS. I wrote this for you! YES, *you*, and I am so excited that you're here. The concept of a "really big Jesus" is something that's been marinating on the inside of me for a while now, and after much prayer, writing, and rewriting, I am delighted to share with you how my eyes have been opened and my heart filled with wonder by seeing and meeting this Jesus that I thought I already knew. Did I mention prayer? What about rewriting? Well, let me just say, it's finally here.

Before we begin, there are a couple things I want to tell you—beliefs I'd like to share, baselines I'd like to establish. The first is this: I believe there is nothing in all of creation that is bigger than Jesus. Throughout our time together, I am going to tell you that over and over again!

The second is that I believe life is Jesus' classroom. I learn more about His character and nature in normal, mundane life circumstances than anywhere else. It's as if He created the world to be the stage from which He would teach us lessons about who He is. However, to sit at one of the desks of this daily classroom, you must be a student of God. For me, as a student in Jesus' classroom of life, I am always looking for Him to teach me about Himself throughout the day. What I have found is that He is everywhere, and the more I look for Him, the more I see that Jesus just isn't that hard to find. He is the world's worst player at hide-and-seek because He actually desires to be found.

For most believers, it's easy to see how big Jesus is in the midst of wild testimonies, yet it can be challenging to see in the middle of great heartache. However, when you're always looking for Him, you begin to realize that everything we go through, whether good or bad, is forming us into the image of Christ. It's in this everyday classroom as a student of God that this grand transformation happens.

This book is a collection of lessons I've learned as I've sat at His desk, and in many ways, I am very much still learning. My hope with these pages is that you feel His invitation to you to enroll as a student of God and join me in looking for Jesus in every area of your life, even if that's in the hard places, the challenges, or the areas that need breakthrough. I would be willing to bet that His fingerprints are all over your life, and even some of the greatest of difficulties you are facing are just opportunities to see our savior as more than all you need. He is a really big Jesus who is able to do more than you can imagine.

In February of 2021, I wrote the poem that's between this prologue and the table of contents. That was the beginning of what would become *Big Jesus*. We had just come out of crazy 2020 where I, just like the rest of the world, watched everything be shaken. Fear ran rampant as the pandemic unleashed on the nations of the world. Injustice paraded itself down the streets of our nation as racism was exposed. Brother was turned against brother as the nation was divided between blue and red political parties. The earth was in an uproar as every eye watched the chaos. Even in the church, it seemed as if most eyes were on all the issues instead of King Jesus. It was as if we had forgotten His might and power. We were bound by fear and in desperate need of a much bigger Jesus than we currently knew.

That is why I started writing. I have a deep conviction that we need a big Jesus in our day and age. Not a Jesus that was reserved only for the early church, but a Jesus who is big today! I also have a conviction that Jesus is the answer to every issue that is on the earth. That's right, every issue. Whether it is big or small, global and local. His name is just too high and His power too strong for Him not to be the solution. However, we don't need a Jesus that we've fashioned into our own image or looks identical to us. You see, we've done that really well in the West. We don't need a Jesus that fits into our religious boxes or paradigms. No, we need the real Jesus. The resurrected King that conquered death. We don't need a Caucasian Jesus who is a patriotic American and looks like a republican or a democrat or any other man-made agenda. We need a Jesus who is stronger than a pandemic and can't be canceled because He isn't politically correct. We need a Jesus that is present in our every day and leads us with His voice. That still small voice that, at even a whisper, is louder than culture's agenda. A Jesus whose love is tangible, and when He shows up, He touches your entire world and every aspect of your life. He leaves nothing unturned. This is the Jesus we read about in the Bible, and when He returns, it won't be some small gesture. No, this Jewish Israeli man will split the sky and every eye will see Him. He will have the sickest tattoo on His thigh and a massive sword in His hand, and everyone will know: He is a really big Jesus. Don't believe me? You can read all about it in Revelation 19 yourself. He is strong and He's mighty, and on that day, every knee will bow before Him, and every tongue will declare that Jesus is Lord.

By the way, I also think it's worth mentioning that these words and pages are not a political statement. They aren't meant to form a theology that can be used like a weapon. No, this entire writing is all about Jesus, simply because the works of His hands are meant to be remembered. His ways are to be boasted in so that faith is built in His people. I am not about debating His gospel or concerning myself with things that are too lofty for me. I simply want to love God and exalt His name. I want to tell you about a man whose ways are so grand and whose love is so large that we get lost forever in wonder. I think that's what was exposed in 2020. In the midst of fear and the unknown, we had lost our wonder and saw other things—issues in our world—as bigger than Jesus.

So, I want to invite you: come wonder with me, and I pray that together we see how alive Jesus still is today! I pray these stories provoke you to look at your own life and find Jesus everywhere. I pray this book will build your faith and give you hope to believe in Him for big things. I pray that as you read these pages, it will cause you to look at your own life and see all the hidden history you have with Him. And I hope it gives you permission to live a life of prayer, giving God the honest and authentic thoughts of your heart. Let's wonder together, but as we wonder, let's be students of God, sitting together in the classroom of life, looking unto Jesus. He is always looking to be found, and He is always teaching us about who He is.

Maybe you are reading this, and you don't know Jesus. Maybe you've heard His name but have never seen His power. If that's you, then my prayer is that this book would open your eyes to see the most loving King, who is zealous for your heart. He is so much more than a God who lives behind the pages of a two-thousand-year-old book. I've found that He leaps right off those pages and unapologetically fills your life with Himself, because this savior who is so big has a deep desire to know and be known by YOU.

So again, welcome. I'm so glad you're here. These are my prayers, my hopes, and my desires as you read. I want to see Him become bigger to you than anything else in this world. Bigger than any problem or issue. Bigger than any mindset or dream you may have. Let's get lost in wonder together and learn from Him. Let's see Him as He really is: a **big Jesus.**

—A

INTERACTIVE PAGE

How do you want Jesus to be BIG in your life?

WRITE HERE

_____

_____

_____

_____

_____

_____

_____

_____

_____

_____

_____

_____

_____

_____

Chapter 1

BIG BOXES

Jesus is just too big to fit in a box!

I 've been walking with Jesus now for about a decade, and what a decade it has been. I would have never thought a life with Jesus would be filled with such excitement, wonder, and fascination. Then again, He is the King of the universe, so I am not sure why I, or anyone, would assume differently. You would think it would be a no-brainer that the One who hung the galaxies like they were a sheet is also big enough to move greatly in our lives. I mean, come on! He created the frequency of the lion's roar, He drew the boundary lines of the ocean's tides, He fashioned you and me down to the exact mole and wrinkle while in our mothers' wombs.

Our King of the universe redeems cities and delivers nations, and the world should know Jesus as He is, extremely big. He is the one who provides all our needs, He restores broken families, and He heals broken bodies. He leads us with His voice, and His leadership far surpasses all others. He holds all authority in His name, and in His hands are the keys of death. The greatest news of the gospel is, in fact, this Jesus we read of in scripture who conquered hell, death, and the grave, and is still alive today and moving on the earth. However, what I have realized is that we often miss seeing Him correctly because of our really big boxes we try to put Him in. Let me explain.

When I was a kid, I woke up one Christmas morning to a present under the Christmas tree that was making a strange noise. Every other present was stationary and silent, yet this one was running around and barking. I had never had a barking Christmas present before, so I was more excited than ever. His name was Sparky. At the time, I was a small kid whose smile would reach all the way from ear to ear. The moment I saw this energetic little dog, I let out a goofy smile that revealed I had just recently lost a few teeth, and with my toothless grin, I immediately decided we would be best friends. Sparky was the type of dog that also had a smile that reached from ear to ear, so we fit together perfectly. We were two buddies that thought life was a playground. Sparky and I would play tug-of-war with the tiny plush toy he came with, and we would chase each other around the house. We would even watch TV together when mom would allow it. For some reason, my favorite thing to do with my new furry friend was to put him in a box and push him around. I am not sure why little boys like to do strange things like put puppies in boxes, but when you're eight years old, it seems like the most exciting idea ever. I would tell Sparky that the box was his own personal dog car as I slid him into it. I'd give him a countdown and then begin to push him across the room! No matter how fast the takeoff or how well I prepped him, we would never make it very far. It seemed as if it was always at the same distance, at the same mark on the floorboard, that Sparky would jump from the box and abandon ship. We would both be out of breath and hearts racing! What a time.

However, pretty soon I learned something about puppies that I didn't know. Puppies grow! It was inevitable that as Sparky grew, so did the boxes I tried to put him in. I would find whatever box I could that was big enough to put my brown fluffy friend in, and as I searched, Sparky was right by my side the entire time. Sometimes we would find a cardboard box and other times it was the laundry basket, but as time went on, it became more and more challenging to find a big enough box. Eventually, Sparky became so big that the boxes I put him in were not strong enough to hold him, and my barking Christmas present would break free. Our dog car days were over. He was bigger than all the boxes I had, and I knew he could no longer fit in one.

As Christians, we do the same with Jesus. I don't mean dog car rides to see how far we can get down the hallway, but I do think we sometimes search far and wide to find a big enough box to put Jesus in. Our boxes for Him come in all different shapes and sizes. These boxes are the frameworks we construct to make sense in our mind how and why God moves the way He does... or sometimes doesn't. Anytime our experience with God outgrows those boxes, then we simply find a bigger box. However, like Sparky, I think it's time we let God smash the boxes we try to put Him in. We have entire denominations and movements built like boxes that often keep us from seeing just how big God really is. We create theologies and really big words to say God doesn't speak or move in certain ways today, but maybe all these constructs are just boxes we put Him in. What if we simply chose to believe that He is bigger than our boxes and a really big Jesus?

In John 4, Jesus tells His disciples that He needs to go to Samaria, the place they have been avoiding all their lives. He has an appointment on His calendar with a lady they don't think He should be meeting with, but since when did Jesus do things based on what we thought is right? So, the disciples go into town to pick up lunch and Jesus heads to the coffee shop for His 1:00 p.m. Kidding, obviously there wasn't such a thing as a coffee shop in 30 AD Samaria. However, Jesus does head to a public well that many would come to and draw water from. Many times, Jesus would go speak to the crowds, but on this occasion, He was just waiting for one. I don't know if He waited for a long time or just for a moment, but eventually the woman came, and when she did, she had one of the most significant conversations with our Lord that has ever happened. In case you are unfamiliar with the passage, here is the account of their conversation:

> *A woman of Samaria came to draw water. Jesus said to her, «Give Me a drink." For His disciples had gone away into the city to buy food. Then the woman of Samaria said to Him, "How is it that You, being a Jew, ask a drink from me, a Samaritan woman?" For Jews have no dealings with Samaritans. Jesus answered and said to her, "If you knew the gift of God, and who it is who says to you, 'Give Me a drink,' you would have asked Him, and He would have given you living water." The woman said to Him, "Sir, You have nothing to draw with, and the well is deep.*

*Where then do You get that living water? Are You **greater** than our father Jacob, who gave us the well, and drank from it himself, as well as his sons and his livestock?" Jesus answered and said to her, "Whoever drinks of this water will thirst again, but whoever drinks of the water that I shall give him will never thirst. But the water that I shall give him will become in him a fountain of water springing up into everlasting life." The woman said to Him, "Sir, give me this water, that I may not thirst, nor come here to draw." Jesus said to her, "Go, call your husband, and come here." The woman answered and said, "I have no husband." Jesus said to her, "You have well said, 'I have no husband,' for you have had five husbands, and the one whom you now have is not your husband; in that you spoke truly." The woman said to Him, "Sir, I perceive that You are a prophet. Our fathers worshiped on this mountain, and you Jews say that in Jerusalem is the place where one ought to worship." Jesus said to her, "Woman, believe Me, the hour is coming when you will neither on this mountain, nor in Jerusalem, worship the Father. You worship what you do not know; we know what we worship, for salvation is of the Jews. But the hour is coming, and now is, when the true worshipers will worship the Father in spirit and truth; for the Father is seeking such to worship Him. God is Spirit, and those who worship Him must worship in spirit and truth." **The woman said to Him, "I know that Messiah is coming" (who is called Christ).***

"When He comes, He will tell us all things." Jesus said
to her, *"I who speak to you am He."* Emphasis added.

John 4:7-26 (NKJV)

Now, this is a famous portion of scripture that you have probably read or heard, but I want to draw your attention to verse 25. We see Jesus the Messiah standing before a woman that knows the prophecy that a messiah will come. She looks at Him and basically says *I know that Messiah is coming and when He does, He will tell me what you're telling me.* What's so profound about this is that the Messiah is right in front of her, and she doesn't even recognize Him. But she's saying that when He comes, she will recognize Him. Funny, right? The one she has been waiting for her entire life is standing right before her and she doesn't even see it! This woman at the well had put God in a box of what it looks like when the Messiah comes. I do not know how she thought He would come, but the way Jesus approached her wasn't it.

The good news is, He is a really big Jesus, and in verse 26 He smashes her box. *"I who speak to you am He."* With this one phrase, He says to her that, if she's willing to smash the framework she has God in, she will see that God himself, the Messiah, whom all of Israel is waiting for, is here engaging her in conversation. If you keep reading the story, you see that she's so shaken by Jesus that she drops her water pot, sprints into town, and starts telling everyone she sees that the Messiah is here. She was willing to smash her box, and, in return, she got Jesus.

There were very few people in the gospels who were willing to do what the Samaritan woman did and put a sledgehammer to her man-made construct of God. It was actually the lack of that very thing that killed Jesus. We can read and see that the Pharisees of the day had big boxes too. I have always been intrigued by the religious leaders of Jesus' day, known as the Sanhedrin. In case you are not familiar with the Pharisees, they were the pastors and church staff in that period. They also had political power in the Roman Empire. However, if you've ever had a run in with harsh rules from a church, well these guys invented them. For the most part, we like to point our fingers at them and call them the bad guys. Whenever we imagine what it would be like if we were in the gospels, we see ourselves as a Peter, full of zeal for God and the boldness to act on it. Or maybe we'd be more like John the beloved, the disciple who laid his head upon Jesus' chest. Perhaps you relate to one of the Sons of Thunder, willing to call down fire on sin and compromise. Possibly, for you it's the disciple Matthew, the tax collector who was a bad guy turned good. Regardless of who it is that you relate to, or where you would find yourself had you been in the narrative of that day, I know who we would NOT want to be: one of the Pharisees. We stick up our noses and denounce any resemblance of them in us. They were stuck in their ways and hardened of heart. They were unwilling to let go of the fact that *surely nothing good comes from Nazareth*. All of that can be summed up in this one phrase: they had really big boxes.

Here is a scary thought: if that day was today, they would no longer be called Pharisees or Sanhedrin, but instead they would be called pastors and worship leaders. As a pastor myself, that is frightening. I must always be looking for the Pharisee in me so I can smash the new boxes I've found. You see, it wasn't the broken and the sinner that didn't receive Jesus. It wasn't the wounded and the sick that sought to kill Him. No, it was those who were supposed to be leading the people to Him. At their core, the only real difference between the disciples and the Pharisees is one set was willing to smash their boxes while the other was not. Both said they loved God, both wanted to lead the people well, and both wanted to see the Kingdom of God come. However, God being born as a baby to a poor virgin girl just didn't fit into the Pharisee's box. God healing the sick in various ways didn't fit either. In fact, raising the dead, dining with sinners, casting out demons, and most of the things performed by Jesus did not fit, and so there was only one solution; Jesus of Nazareth must be killed. That's what boxes do to you, they steal your wonder and fascination with who Jesus is. Instead of marveling at Him and seeing His beauty, in the face of what you did not know about Him, you pick up stones to stone Him! I will tell you more about throwing stones in the coming chapters.

You can always tell when someone has a bigger box than a big Jesus because they look more like a skeptic than a believer. Believers are supposed to believe. I never understood how you can have a believer who doesn't believe, but trust me, they are out there.

In John 14, Jesus is preparing His disciples for His death. He is about to die at the hands of the Sanhedrin, and soon after that He will rise from the dead and ascend back to Heaven. Of course, the disciples know none of what is about to take place.

In fact, they have expectations in their hearts that Jesus is going to overthrow the Roman government and establish His physical kingdom in Israel. That day will come! However, it wouldn't be in the disciples' lifetime, so what Jesus is about to say to them seems like a riddle. It just doesn't quite fit into their box of what they think is supposed to happen. He tells them many things, but in John 14:12, Jesus says this:

> *Most assuredly, I say to you, he who believes in Me, the works that I do he will do also; and **greater works than these he will do**, because I go to my Father. And whatever you ask in My name, that I will do, that the Father may be glorified in the Son. If you ask anything in My name, I will do it. If you love Me, keep My commandments. And I will pray the Father, and He will give you another **Helper, that He may abide with you forever**. (Emphasis added)*

Jesus is informing His followers that He is going away and that it is actually better for mankind that He does, for the Holy Spirit is about to come. Now, this isn't a book about the Holy Spirit, but if it were, I would tell you all about how the Holy Spirit is God and how His favorite thing to do is reveal Jesus to us. He loves to highlight the work of His hands and show us how near Jesus is each and every day. I have found that the Holy Spirit helps us to see that the revelation of Jesus is EVERYWHERE. Simply put, you can see Jesus everywhere and in everything with the Holy Spirit! He reveals Christ! I find Him in conversations with dear friends. I find Him outside in nature, in trees, rivers, and mountains. I find Jesus in setbacks and trials and in the hard times. That is what the Holy Spirit does; He shows us Jesus. It is His absolute favorite thing to do. Believers who believe are always looking for Jesus. They are not skeptical or critical. They are not blaming things on coincidence, but quite the contrary. They are believing for GREATER things and looking for Jesus in everything.

However, this isn't a book about Holy Spirit. Maybe another day I will write one, but this is a book about Jesus and how big He is, even today in the twenty-first century. In verse twelve, Jesus says, "He who believes in me." If you are reading this, I am going to assume you believe in Jesus. If you do not, then by the end of it, I pray that you do. I pray your heart is pounding with faith, and by the Holy Spirit's leadership, you see that Jesus is too big to be put in a box and that He loves you dearly.

> *"Most assuredly,"* He says, *"He who believes in me* (That's you)*, the works that I do he will do also; and **greater** works than these he will do..."* (Emphasis added)

Isn't that amazing? Think of all the fascinating stories and amazing miracles of the Bible and wonderful signs Jesus performed; these are the "works" He is referring too. Now, once you think you've begun to scratch the surface of imagining all He has done, imagine greater! This "greater" won't only come by the hands of Jesus but through the lives of those who believe in Him.

I am not one to give fancy lessons on Hebrew words and original writings of scripture, but I am going to do my best to try to explain what Jesus is saying here. So here we go! The Greek word used for "greater works" is the word *megas*. It means this: *More mass in weight, more length in height, larger volume in space, more numerous in number, more intensity in degree.* It truly is greater all around, both in quality and quantity. This is what Jesus is talking about to the disciples: the life that believers who believe live, a life of mega, or more! This is also what I believe Paul is referring to in his letter to the church in Ephesus. In Ephesians 3:20 he writes:

> *Now to Him who is able to do **exceedingly abundantly above all that we ask or think**, according to the power that works in us, to Him be glory in the church by Christ Jesus to all generations, forever and ever. Amen. Emphasis added.*

Believers who believe are looking for the greater, the more than we can ask or even think. I don't know about you, but I can think of some pretty big and wild things. I usually don't ask as big as I am thinking in my mind. Jesus probably knows that we often water down our "asks," so He addresses it head on like a bulldozer. It's as if He has put a challenge before us saying, "I bet you can't think up things to ask that are bigger than I am." We could have entire brainstorming meetings to think of bigger things and He would still outdo us. This is the kind of faith we need today. This is the kind of faith that believers who believe in a big Jesus have.

In my early days of following Jesus, I used to pin many things on coincidence. But when you choose to live a life of faith, coincidence no longer exists. As I look back on my history with Him, I now see how He was hidden in every detail of my life, and little coincidences were actually little kisses from Heaven. Like when we get a random phone call from a relative we were just thinking about the day before. Or when you constantly see that same number on a license plate while you are out in public. For my wife, beautiful Sarahbeth, she seems to always run into the same blue jay on days she needs encouragement. Some would say coincidence, but believers who believe call it the "greater." We have a phrase around the community I live in for moments that don't make sense to our minds. It goes like this: "That's weird! Could be God. It probably is." This phrase is like a safeguard that keeps us from constructing new boxes and helps us see a big Jesus. It takes moments of coincidence and turns them into kisses from Heaven. I have had a lot of kisses from Heaven since I started following Jesus, and if I had to put money on it, I bet you have too.

The following chapters are stories that are just that! Kisses from Heaven. They are stories of the "greater" that will confront our boxes that we put Him in. I say *our* because my own boxes have been smashed time and time again, and I am sure there is more smashing to come. However, that's the beautiful thing about being a believer who believes - you get to smash your boxes and keep your wonder and fascination with who Jesus is. As you read these chapters, you might find yourself saying things like, "That's weird!" If you do, maybe you follow it up with "Could be God. Probably is!" and perhaps you'll see a really big Jesus. I also pray that it leaves you believing for "greater" in your own life. Revelation 19:10 says: *"Worship God! For the testimony of Jesus is the spirit of prophecy."*

The testimony of Jesus is the spirit of prophecy. Wow! If it's a testimony of Jesus and what He has done or what He is like, then it's a prophecy of who He will be or what He will do for someone else. It may be that you don't know what to do with words like prophecy. So let me say it like this; If He did it for me, and if He is big enough to do it for someone else, then He can do it for you! For the testimony of Jesus is the spirit of prophecy! After all, He is the King of the universe, and He is a really big Jesus who won't fit in even the biggest of boxes.

"Jesus, thank you that you want to be known by me and you want to show me your ways. As I read these pages, I ask you to smash any boxes that I have put you in. Would you give me the faith to live as a believer who believes that YOU are more than able to do all that I think, ask, or imagine?"

Chapter 2

WATERSOUND

The love of Jesus will not hesitate to knock you down!

My wife and I recently had our first child, and we are over the top in love with our sweet little Rosie. She's all smiles, always, and she gives them out to anyone she sees. You always hear people talk about how there is no love that compares to the type of love a parent has for their child, but it just doesn't click until the day your own sweet little Rosie comes. In a moment, it all hits you—an unbelievably overwhelming love. It is as if your heart is suddenly wide open and there is a new and fresh flowing river right down the center of it. It feels refreshing, it feels strong, and with no hesitation, it knocks you down. The second I laid eyes on sweet little Rosie, I thought, *I will do anything for you!* I would give up any dreams or desire, and I would pay any amount of money to make sure she is safe and healthy. I would lay my own life down for this beautiful little girl. It's the craziest feeling ever! I have always been the type of guy that loves to do the extreme stuff. Like jump out of an airplane strapped to someone with a parachute or bungee jump off a bridge just for the rush of it. I am pretty sure I have conquered every roller coaster and every thrilling adventure I have ever come face to face with, but none of these feats compares to the rush of overwhelming love.

It reminds me of someone else who willingly laid down their life for mankind. And no, I am not referring to the way Iron Man iconically snapped his fingers. I am talking about Jesus. Who, for the joy set before Him, endured the cross, despising the shame. If I had to give His love a number, I wouldn't say it's 3,000, I would say it's more like three trillion. That joy that was set before Him was you and I intimately knowing Him and knowing His love, the overwhelming kind. We all know that *"God so loved the world He gave His only Son!"* To be honest, we know it a little too well. John 3:16 has become the verse we have on pillows and inside pictures frames, but often we don't have it inside our hearts. What I mean is, maybe we have it memorized, but the real question is do we live with the conviction that we are loved by God? It is sad, really, that the phrase "Jesus loves you" has become a cliché thing to say, even in the church. However, believers who believe know that the love of Jesus will not hesitate to knock you down. In fact, Jesus loves to lavish His love upon us. That three-word phrase, *Jesus loves you*, is actually one of the most profound statements one can make, and if you let it, it will smash any box you may have. Sometimes smashing boxes is as simple as allowing your heart to know what your head knows. I always know when I have constructed a new box around His love because that three-word phrase stops moving my heart. It is in those moments that I must slow down and really remind my heart, *"Aaron, Jesus loves you!"* Isn't that true love, anyways? Not that we love God, but that He loves us.

A few months before sweet little Rosie would open her eyes and take her first breath, we decided to make the best of our final moments as a couple expecting their first child, and we made the effort to get away on a babymoon. If you don't know, a babymoon is similar to a honeymoon in that it is a celebratory vacation. However, instead of spending time alone with your spouse after getting married, you're spending quality time together before the birth of a new baby. The point is to spend one last hurrah together before things get crazy and your lives and schedule dramatically change. For those of you thinking of having a baby, let me say that again: your lives and schedules dramatically change. But don't worry, it's all for the better! (Insert wink emoji here.)

After much debate and discussion, we finally made our decision of where we would take this last hurrah as a childless couple: WaterSound beach, Florida. WaterSound is a small community off the Gulf of Mexico on highway 30A. The Beaches are stark white while the water is a hydrating blue, and the two seem as if they perfectly dance together. We had a room that overlooked the tide as it rolled in, and for the next four days, we would do nothing except soak in the sun.

Now, I want to take a moment to tell you about Sarahbeth. To me, she is beyond beautiful. I don't just mean in looks, although she is stunningly gorgeous. I way outdid myself and I am still not sure how I got her to go on that first date with me. What I am referring to is who she is on the inside. She's a believer who believes, and most of the stories you will read about have her smack right in the middle of them. They are some of the greatest moments we've experienced together where God showed up as really big in the middle of our small lives. Nonetheless, even in the midst of mighty breakthroughs, marriage is challenging, and often the word I would probably choose to describe it is *hard*. Yet I say she is beyond beautiful because in the midst of the challenges of marriage, I continually watch Sarahbeth lay her life down for me and our family. No matter the disagreement or misunderstanding, she regularly chooses to express forgiveness, repentance, and kindness. She fights to keep her heart open and always strives to see the best in other people. Especially those that are closest to her. She loves God deeply, and she daily chooses Jesus to be her first love. In fact, a lot of who I know Jesus to be I've learned from her. Sarahbeth has this way of believing in people that causes them to believe in themselves. She never backs down from a challenge and doesn't boast when she accomplishes it. She makes hard things fun, and that's why to me, she's *beautiful Sarahbeth*. You'll see me refer to her that way from here on out. The Bible says that he who finds a wife finds a good thing. Well, she is my good thing and even though our marriage has been very far from perfect, and at times we've even had to seek wisdom and council, I am madly, and deeply in love with my beautiful bride. Anyways, back to the story. Where was I? Soaking in the sun...

Beautiful Sarahbeth and I have a unique situation. She isn't overly fond of the sand and would lie out at the pool from open to close if she had it her way. If I had it my way, I would build sandcastles, and just as the sun started to feel a little too much, I would run into the ocean to be pounded by the incoming waves. I would switch back and forth between beach and water until the sun went to bed. However, marriage is an expert at killing *"your way*," so we have adapted to a healthy middle, and we put together a plan. In the morning we went to the beach. I got to build my sandcastles and explore the ocean floor, searching for strange things like crabs and seashells. Sarahbeth would break out one of the many books she was currently reading, while listening to the crashing of waves as she sat under her umbrella. When lunch time arrived, we'd pack up our things, rinse off under the freshwater fountain, and head to the restaurant by the pool for lunch. After lunch, we'd take to the pool! This was the time of day when Sarahbeth would normally choose to swim with me, there in the boujee water, as I called it. Although, on several occasions, I talked her into the ocean. I even sometimes talked her into exploring the pool floor with me, similar to the way I hunt for animal life in the ocean, but we've yet to find anything exotic at the bottom of the pool. In the late afternoon, we usually cleaned up as nicely as we could and ventured to the side of town with the best restaurants. It was four days of paradise filled with sun, swimming, good food, and, most importantly, quiet intentional time before our sweet little Rosie would bring spice to our life. Side note: I am Hispanic, so a life with spice is a life that's nice.

On our final full day at WaterSound, we stuck to the usual. Beach. Lunch. Pool. However, my bride was feeling a little adventurous, and she thought it would be fun to do one final dip in the ocean before calling it a day. Of course, I was all in. "Say less!" I quickly exclaimed as she brought forth the idea. I hopped out of the chlorine filled water and gathered our things as quickly as I could. I had to get us moving and on our way before she changed her mind. We hurried down the boardwalk and onto the beaming sand. By the time we reached the shore, we could feel the sweat sliding down our arms and we both jumped into the first wave we saw. That is really the way we've chosen to live our lives anyways, fully jumping into whatever it is we're doing. We both feel like it's really the only way to live, especially if you are desiring to live a life of faith. Sometimes you get knocked down, but I'd rather be in the wave than be watching it. There is no room for boxes in the wave, they'll just get swept away.

We had only been in the water for five minutes when I discovered I had run into the waves so quickly I had forgotten to empty out my pockets. Luckily, the only thing I had in my shorts was our room key and a debit card. I was so surprised they didn't wash out because the pockets on my shorts were small and open. I made sure to grab them and run them to our pile of belongings on the beach and head back to enjoy the final minutes swimming around with my pregnant bride.

Our final evening would look different than most. Before our dinner reservations, we would be shuttled to the car rental spot to pick up a vehicle we would need to get to the airport the following morning. It would be quick. We made sure to do all the logistics online so it would be a hassle-free pick up. As you know, most people only have hassle-free experiences with car rental companies, so we had no reason to worry. Upon arrival, all we needed was a credit card and an ID that matched, both in the name of who the car was reserved under. We quickly arrived, and as I approached the employee working the front desk, I heard his clear instructions. "I need to see your credit card and driver's license, please."

"No problem." I responded as I reached for my cards. I knew exactly where in my bag I had placed them earlier as I ran them out of the salty water. I unzipped my backpack, reaching in to remove my credit card and ID.

So strange. I thought. They should've both been in my bag, but only my credit card was inside. My ID was not. I was slow to panic as I knew it had to be around here somewhere. Before I knew it, my entire backpack was dumped on the counter of the company, and in the midst of the mess, my driver's license was missing in action. I thought back through the day, trying my best to remember the last place I had it. Isn't that the technique all the experts say to use when you've misplaced something? And by experts, I mean the loved ones in your life who are doing their best to help you find what's been lost. You think back to the last time you had it.

"Think. Think. Think, Aaron," I mumbled to myself as I replayed the day in my mind. Pretty quickly, a memory was flashing through my brain. It was in the pile of cards I rushed into my pocket as we made our way from poolside to beach. There was only one solution. It had slipped out of that small and open pocket in my swimsuit as we played in the waves. I was now in the middle of a first world catastrophe. I needed to get our rental, and about sixteen hours later catch a flight, and here I was with no ID. SOS! I don't know if you've ever rented a car before but let me state that my earlier comment about it being hassle free was full on sarcasm. Even with everything you need, it seems as if it can still be tricky. Without what you need, you can forget about it! It's like trying to make it through TSA without identification, which, by the way, if you haven't realized it, that was problem number two to figure out. Even if I somehow got the rental, how would I get through airport security and make it onto the plane with no ID?

I'll spare you the details, because it wasn't a fun experience, but about an hour and half later, four transfers up through higher management, and lots of pleading, we finally got a rental car. In the midst of all of that, we missed our dinner reservations. For our final night of "paradise" we would be picking up pizza. Just for the record: it didn't have pineapple on it. We did pretend it was a five-star dinner and broke out the soda to make it a TV dinner. Why not? We were on vacation. It only took about one slice in for me to hijack dinner and ask the question, "What are we going to do?" It was great that we had made the best of the evening and all, but let's address the elephant in the room. Tomorrow was going to have its challenges. Without my ID, we could forget catching our flight.

The next words to come out of my bride were not what I was expecting. "Why don't we pray and ask the Lord to help us find it?" I wasn't sure if we were now telling jokes, or if maybe she knew something about Jesus that I didn't. I now know that it was the latter. Her comment was exposing a box and inviting me to see a big Jesus.

"Yeah, we could!" I responded, more annoyed than anything by the absurd notion that Jesus would just make my ID reappear like we were living a sci-fi movie. It was easy to tell that I had zero faith for something like that, and even if the world's strongest microscope was actually able to discover even the tiniest sliver of it, it had to be no bigger than a little mustard seed. The thing is, I just didn't realize what Jesus could do with mustard seed size faith. Even on a beach in WaterSound. Not paying attention to my negative attitude, Sarahbeth had another idea.

"You could call David and ask him to pray."

Now, let me you tell you about my friend David. He is the type of guy whose faith makes you wonder, and the way he knows Jesus makes you feel like something just isn't quite right with him, or maybe something is too right. Regardless, he knows overwhelming love and he knows the only One who can author it. David is a believer who believes. In the early days of our friendship, we both served in youth ministry together. We often found ourselves in unusual circumstances and wild environments while working with teenagers. It's just that way when you are in youth ministry. Sometimes you find yourself sleeping under the stars next to a handful of sophomore boys in the middle of summer. Other times you are playing Xbox, trying your best not to let a middle schooler whoop you in "Madden." It's usually always an interesting experience. On one specific outing, we were spending winter break out of town at a several day worship event, and it happened to be during the heat of the college football playoffs. So, of course we had to spend our lunch break squeezing in as much of the fourth quarter as we could. David busted out his laptop, got the game on the screen, and we all crowded around to see what would happen. Immediately, one of the boys pointed to the red battery icon on the upper right corner of the screen. The computer had only five percent battery. We had no charger, no spare laptop, and no ideas. In the midst of scrambling around trying to figure out what to do, we heard David grab everyone's attention.

"Watch this," He said, as he laid his hands on his laptop and began to pray for the battery to be charged. This is exactly what I mean when I say something isn't right with my friend. However, we all lost our minds and began to freak out as we watched the battery percentage on the screen climb from five percent to six, and then jump to seven without being plugged into any charger. "It's by faith!" David exclaimed through his full-on joyous laugh. And this is exactly what I mean when I say maybe something is too right with him. He is full of faith for even outrageous things. I was present with him another time when he lost his wallet in the nearby lake, and a full week later, he found it when we were out swimming around. That morning, he had prayed and asked Jesus to help him find it, and sure enough, he did. Call it coincidence if you'd like, but if you talk to David, he will tell you faith is a lot more powerful than we think. He has no boxes to put Jesus in because he knows just how big He really is. Now, back to the conversation during our TV dinner. I don't remember what my chat with David looked like or if the phone call even went through, but that didn't really matter. At just the thought of David's wild stories, it gave me enough hope to believe that if Jesus had done it for him, then He could do it for me. Remember, the testimony of Jesus is the spirit of prophecy!

We grabbed hands and began to pray the simplest prayer we could, asking Jesus to help us find my driver's license. Beautiful Sarahbeth suggested we go on one last walk down the shoreline the next morning and see if it would turn up. I agreed, and just as the sun had finished rising, we were out the door and headed back towards the waves. My pregnant bride had so much excitement as she was full of faith that the card was going to turn up. Just as we approached the spot where we had been swimming the day before, I took a deep breath and tried my best to stop thinking about the consequences that would ensue at the airport if it didn't turn up.

Jesus, if you love me, you'll help me find my ID, I silently said to the Lord in my mind. Instantly, that thought was followed by conviction. I had too much history with Jesus to be questioning if He loved me. I quickly repented and moved on, hoping my proof of identification was just a few steps away. We searched all up and down the shoreline for the next twenty minutes looking in the sand and even in the shallow tide, while each passing minute brought more and more disappointment. I would love to be able to tell you that I ran into an angel that was super jacked and had muscles as big as my head and magically floated over to me with my ID in hand. I'm not sure that's what angels look like, but it's pretty cool to imagine. However, that's not what happened. Not even close. My ID was nowhere to be found. We decide to throw in the towel and head to the car. As we began to part ways with the sea, we started dreaming of all the possible solutions that could play out at the airport. However it played out, it was sure to be eventful. Just as we were about to exit the sand, we noticed a beach boy setting up umbrellas and chairs in the sand for the morning rush.

It's worth a shot, I thought as I headed his way to see if anyone had turned in my ID. It was a Hail Mary chance, but at least the hope was still alive. I got his attention and asked if they had a driver's license in the lost and found. What he said next destroyed my box.

"Actually, I found one this morning! Let's go see if that's it!" He shouted. He quickly jogged over to his cabana and came running to me with a Texas driver's license in his hand.

"You're never going to believe this, but I found it in the water this morning washed up on shore! The tide was soon to carry it back out!" He handed me the ID and it had my name on it. Literally. There was even a picture on it to match my face. I was in disbelief. The card I was holding in my hand had just slept overnight in the ocean and washed back up on shore. That simple prayer we prayed the night before all of sudden didn't seem so small. And neither did Jesus. As I stared at the card, it was like I could hear His still small voice in my heart. "*I love you.*"

Maybe I had history with Him, but that didn't stop Him from lavishing me with His overwhelming love, and once again it knocked me down. Later that day we got on the airplane hassle free, and we parted ways with WaterSound.

Now, I am not saying that faith is the answer to finding every lost marble that's rolled under the bed or prayer will somehow transport your suitcase that was lost by the airline to the destination it's supposed to be at. I am also not saying prayer can't do that. However, what I am saying is that I had a box around what He could do, and He shattered it. I am also saying His love is really big and Jesus will waste no opportunity to lavish it on you. I think there are a lot of people out there who have lost their ID and are frantically searching for it. Maybe it isn't their physical driver's license like it was for me, but I do know that Jesus is in the business of helping people find their lost identities, and His favorite way to do it is with overwhelming love that knocks you down. Trust me, He will not hesitate to do it. There is something about His love that has a way of cutting through every wall and barrier in your life and speaking directly to the core of who you are. The love of Jesus alters you and removes every insecurity that would have you bound.

In Ephesians 3, Paul is talking about this very thing. In verse 17, he is addressing believers and he says this:

> *That Christ may dwell in your hearts through faith; that you, being rooted and grounded in love, may be able to comprehend with all the saints what is the width and length and depth and height—to know the love of Christ which passes knowledge; that you may be filled with all the fullness of God.*

Paul is saying that we haven't yet come to know how deep His love is, and just in case you think you know it, I am not sure if it is longer than it is deep, or deeper than it is long. It's too high to climb and too wide to cross. It is absolutely overwhelming. His love doesn't make sense and it surpasses all knowledge. Some may even call it reckless. The love of Jesus is what believers who believe are supposed to be rooted in. It's the only soil that will turn a seed into a tree. Without being rooted in His love, that seed just becomes a weed.

The overwhelming love of Jesus is for you and it's for me. His love is for new believers and those who've known Him for decades. It's for the lost and the outcast, it is even for that wild aunt we all have that lives on the other side of the country. You can always tell when someone encounters the overwhelming love of Jesus; it will turn the hardest hearts soft and the most bitter of people into laughing machines. His love also has a way of restoring your lost identity in the very moment it knocks you down, and once you get up, you will never walk the same. Maybe you don't know this, but you were created for love. You exist for God to lavish His love on you. This love that is patient and is kind, you can't earn it and you can't lose it, that is why it's overwhelming. His love is so much more than a thing for your head to know, it's like a wave for your heart to be hit by. And if you've been hit by it, I am sure you're still knocked down. I don't know that you ever get up once you're hit by the love of God. I think it totally discombobulates you and causes you to live differently for the rest of your days. I think it's because it comes like wave after wave. The love of Jesus isn't a onetime experience, but it's day, after day, after day. Sometimes if we ever realize we're somehow standing on two feet again, and we've grown numb to that phrase "*Jesus loves you*," it's just an indicator that we need to get hit by another wave of overwhelming love. It'll totally knock you down. Sometimes it's scary, but it's better to be in the wave than watching it.

If, somehow, you seem to have misplaced your identity and you don't know what to do to find it, or maybe you've yet to be knocked down by love (if you had, you would know), I dare you to believe He is a big Jesus and pray a simple prayer like, "*Lord, will you help me find my ID.*" See what becomes with just a little bit of faith. Maybe you'll run into an angel with muscles the size of your head, or maybe even in the midst of all your history with Jesus He will whisper again to you "*I love you.*" Who knows, you might even run into a beach boy who finds your identity in the sea. Perhaps one day you'll get to meet David and the two of you can swap stories of outrageous faith. Regardless of the outcome and all the events that take place, I bet you end up like me, knocked down, and you find yourself in the wave of overwhelming love.

"Jesus, thank you for your love. Would you break any boxes I have around the love that you have for me. Would you speak identity over me and root me and ground me in your love? Give me the faith to live with my identity being found only in YOU!"

Chapter 3

TURN OFF THE PUMP

It's a worry-free zone under Jesus' leadership!

At the end of every year, beautiful Sarahbeth and I celebrate our anniversary. We tied the knot on New Year's Eve, so we quite literally do it on the final day of the year. The whole world is celebrating, so we are always guaranteed a party. And when it comes to celebrating, we like to do it big. In fact, we have a dream to celebrate every year by traveling to either a "Land," a "Ville," or a "Port." Let me break it down for you. We love traveling. In fact, we even put in our vows "Where you go, I go." I mean, come on, the world isn't going to see itself! There's enough worry and care in this life and we've found that one of the best ways to keep an open heart is to see another culture. Plus, Jesus said to go unto all the world! So even He advises that it is worth seeing. However, seeing the world is no small feat. There are a lot of places to see and the opportunities are endless. We want to see them all, and to us, it doesn't really matter how it happens. So, the question is not *where to go*, but *how to make it special*. We put our creative hearts together and brainstormed how we would make it unique to us. We came up with "Land, Ville, and Port." We always choose a new place, and the location has to have one of those three words in its name. For instance, if we wanted to go to Rhode Island we would have to stay in *Newport*. If the selection was an amusement park, then California's *Disneyland* is a great choice. Tennessee is off the books, unless we are going to *Nashville*. Hopefully you are starting to catch on. This is rule number one when celebrating our love.

We have found that the older you get, the quicker the years go by, but it never fails that even in the speed of things, there is always so much to recap and process from the previous twelve months. We always look back at the year and talk about our victories and challenges and then we dream together for the upcoming one. In the midst of this, we are sure to laugh a ton and find some sort of wild thing to do together on our out-of-town adventure. We leave every care at home and put strict boundaries to not discuss anything that will invite worry into our time. Besides, all worry really is, is dreaming, in the negative sense anyways. If you are someone who worries a lot, I would tell you that you are a dreamer. You're just dreaming negatively, that's why it comes out as worry. So, for us, we choose to dream in the positive and believe that the best is yet to come. Too many believers put Jesus in a box with a label called *worry*, and trust me, on many occasions that has been me. My box labeled worry is really big, but that's why I need a bigger Jesus. Worry seems to magnify what may never be, while at the same time shrinking who Jesus is. It isn't that Jesus actually becomes smaller. Oh no! He is far grander than we can imagine. He has no rival, and He has no equal. He is higher than any other name and He is established forever. He can't get any smaller and that's just the way it is. So it isn't that He gets smaller, it's just that we stop being believers who believe and start worrying about what's to come.

In Mark chapter 4, Jesus again is teaching, and this time He is sharing a parable. He likens believers' hearts to four different types of soils and faith to a seed. He explains how the sower sows the seed, and whichever soil the seed falls on will dictate what happens next. It's all about the condition of the soil. I have always wondered how two people could hear the same sermon and one be transformed while the other is numb to what they just heard. How two people can read the same passage of scripture and one person can respond by changing the way they live their life and the other forget what they just read moments after. In this parable, Jesus is explaining that it's all about the soil in which the seed falls. It isn't determined by how well one speaks or preaches, and it won't be determined on what translation you read. It is all about the soil. If you don't know, *the soil* represents our hearts. One of the soils in Mark 4 is the soil of thorns. Jesus says that the seed falls and sprouts, but because of the thorns, the crop is choked, and it bears no fruit. The disciples come to Jesus after the crowd leaves, and they ask Him to breakdown what He was talking about. In verse 18, He explains the thorns.

> *Now these are the ones sown among thorns; they are the ones who hear the word, **and the cares of this world,** the deceitfulness of riches, and the desires for other things entering in choke the word, and it becomes unfruitful. Emphasis added*

The thorns are the cares of this world. In other words, because they couldn't stop worrying and dreaming in the negative, they bore no fruit. Believers who believe are known by their fruit. Jesus is very clear that we don't have to argue or debate our case. We don't need to present what we believe or hold lecture sessions. We need to bear fruit. Fruit speaks for itself, and no one can question fruit. In fact, people eat fruit. But if the cares of this life and worry are choking out your fruit, no one will be able to eat from your life and see through you just how big Jesus really is. I don't know about you, but I want to bear much fruit. One of the places I want to bear that fruit is in my marriage. So "Land, Ville, and Port" are carefree zones. We are not allowed to worry whenever we embark on one of these adventures and this is rule number two.

About halfway through our first year, we started discussing where we wanted to go for our first anniversary celebration. We went to dinner and dreamed of the perfect destination until finally we landed on a spot. We were going to go to Iceland. We had seen a short video that was shot in Iceland, and we instantly wrote its name at the top of our bucket list. If you are unaware, there are two main islands in the Northern Atlantic and Iceland is the one with very little ice. It is beautiful and lush, full of waterfalls and natural hot springs. It would be the perfect destination to celebrate our first year, and we were extremely excited but had much to figure out. The problem we were facing was that money was tight. We were ballin' on a budget, so if we were going to do it, then we would have to find a way to make it affordable. The question we were asking wasn't "Can we do it? but "How are we going to do it?" So we sat down with our financial spreadsheet and we knew exactly what numbers we had to stick to if we were going to make it happen. I would regularly check flight prices and they were anything but cheap. Instead of losing heart, I just kept checking until one day it seemed to all come together. It was my normal routine of checking all airlines via Google flights and this just happened to be our lucky day. We found two flights roundtrip for under $400. What a steal! We booked our flights, got a place to stay, and in a matter of moments our dream was no longer a fantasy. It was an upcoming trip on the calendar.

On our way to the airport, we were giddy as ever. We carried on our bags and watched movies while we laughed together for the entire eleven-hour red-eye, and before we knew it, we were through Customs and on the ground. We were exhausted and grungy, but we didn't let that stop us. We picked up our rental and headed straight for the capital city of Reykjavík. It was beautiful, and the scenery was breathtaking. It was a perfect mix of black lava sand and flourishing green shrubs. There were volcanoes and pseudo-craters covered in steam and geysers that exploded when you stared too long. Then, to top it all off, the Northern lights fill the sky like nothing you've ever seen. We felt like we had fallen off the face of the earth and into an exotic wonderland. We spent the entire first day exploring the city. I think we went to every boutique that was open and then we ended our city rush with a coffee watching the crashing waves as they hit the downtown dam.

Something unique to Iceland is that, if you are going to get the full experience, it requires a hefty amount of driving. We had several landmarks we wanted to see and over the period of three days, we would spend just under twenty hours in the car. The rental we got from the international dealer was a red Hyundai i10. It was smaller than anything we had ever been in before but sure packed a punch. Driving this stick shift machine through the gorgeous mountain roads had me feeling like I belonged in something like the *Italian Job*. Sarahbeth had never driven a manual transmission before, so I decided this would be the moment her amazing husband of one year would come to the rescue and teach her a lifelong skill that she would use forever. About thirty minutes into the lesson, I was praying over the car hoping the clutch hadn't burnt up and that this lesson wasn't going to cost us a fat fee. Once we came to the conclusion that our little red friend was going to be okay, we switched seats and it was off to the next site.

We stopped to hit the grocery store and stock up on food. It would be easy to eat as we drove, and it would save us money from having to eat out. We walked around the store trying to make our selection but quickly things got very interesting. Everything was written in Icelandic, so we weren't sure if we were buying yogurt or sour cream. It was quite a scene the next morning as we timidly took the first bite of our homemade parfaits. However, we were in the clear. It was yogurt.

The first site on our list that day was a place called Glacier Lagoon on Diamond Beach. The locals called it Jökulsárlón. I dare you to try and pronounce that! Glacier Lagoon is a small lake that rests at the edge of Europe's largest ice cap, a stunning and massive glacier. The blue waters are sprinkled with icebergs of all sizes, and if that isn't cool enough, there are hundreds of seals that play all throughout the lagoon. It looks just like a scene out of an old James Bond movie. At the end of the lake, there is a small river that carries the smaller more broken-down iceberg pieces into the Atlantic Ocean. The black sand beach there is known as Diamond Beach because many fragments of ice wash up on the shore, and as the sun hits the coast, it creates the illusion that the ice is actually diamonds. It's even more beautiful than it sounds. As we traveled to the day's destination, we found ourselves stopping multiple times to enjoy the terrain, but I think it was really just an excuse to enjoy each other's company. We would take pictures and skip rocks down rivers we came across. We were in no hurry and had no schedule to follow. On one of our many stops, we saw a herd of sheep standing around grazing in a field. Just as we started to walk their way, a truck pulled into the field about a hundred yards away. An elderly man stepped out and walked around to the back of his pickup and pulled out a large basket full of food. He began to yell something that we didn't understand, and just as he did, all the sheep began to baa in the same tone as they charged to the man. He was their shepherd and he'd come to care for them. The flock consisted of probably thirty sheep, and they all galloped to the shepherd as soon as he lifted his voice. Not one stayed behind. There was, however, one that was a little slower than the rest, but we watched as the shepherd made sure to feed the slow lamb just like all the rest. It was profound, really. We had been yelling at the flock for several minutes and they seemed to not have a care in the world, but the moment their shepherd yelled, they responded. They knew their shepherd's voice. Beautiful Sarahbeth and I laughed about how the sheep knew rule number two and they were reminding us of the conditions of our trip.

As our Icelandic adventure started to come to an end, we began making preparations to get back to the capital city. Our trip had landed us about four hours to the far east side of the island where we had stayed in a remote Airbnb. Our red getaway car was down to fumes in his tank, so we pulled into the nearest gas station to fill up before we would say goodbye to our little Hyundai travel buddy. Just as I went to slide the nose of the line into the car, I noticed that I had never seen a gas pump like this before. You had to turn it on before you inserted your card to pay. I watched the traveler at the pump across the way so I could see how it was done. I mimicked his actions and got the gas flowing. It was different than any way I had ever pumped gas in the past, but I felt like I was getting a taste of the full culture. I pulled out the end of the hose and reinserted it to its home and we pulled out. We were a little behind schedule and we had quite a drive before we would reach the airport. Upon arrival it was go time. Nobody likes to miss a flight, but you especially don't want to miss an international one. We returned the car as quickly as we could and raced through the terminal to get to our gate. It was a buzzer beater moment as we arrived just in time.

As I took my seat, I pulled out my phone and my notepad to balance our expenses and make sure we stayed within budget. If my math was correct, we should be good. I fired up our financial apps and started the assessment.

"Oh no…" I quickly let out. It was the kind of "oh no" that's mixed with shock and instant dread. There was an unknown transaction that was for more than even our plane tickets.

What is this? I nervously thought. I checked the date and searched for the name of the vendor. It was for that same day just a few hours prior. The name of the vendor was the Icelandic gas station we had been at just earlier that morning. Instantly rule number two was out the window. Starting to panic, I grabbed my bride's attention as worry flowed from my lips. "What happened? This doesn't make sense!" I nervously began to question and tried to make sense of what had happened. When you're newlyweds, one of the toughest challenges is learning the dynamics of money, budgeting, and financial teamwork. When money is tight, it seems as if everything is tight. The temptation is to let money become emotional and in turn, become life's biggest worry. Worry leads to fear and fear will lead you to some pretty irrational thinking. Before you know it, you're homeless in your mind and you're imagining a life where you haven't eaten in days. That's how worry works. Remember, it's just like dreaming, but in a negative sense. It causes you to create a narrative and leads you to some funny places in your mind.

As my worry started to draw attention, I heard a voice coming from a neighboring passenger that apparently had more Icelandic experience than me. It seemed he had overheard our conversation and was going to help bring resolve to this mysterious expense.

"Did you turn off the pump?" He asked in a deep, melancholy voice. "If you didn't turn off the pump then you probably paid for the gas of the travelers behind you." The man continued. He went on the explain that one of the many unique aspects to the stunning world of Iceland is that many of the gas stations require you to turn off the pump after use. Failure to do so would mean that the vehicle that comes behind you would have the option to either fill up on your dime or turn off the pump and restart it under their own wallet. Apparently, the lucky contestants after us chose to be blessed that day. And by the size of the bill, they apparently weren't driving a little Hyundai i10. It was probably something more like a multiple bedroom RV. I can still imagine them giggling with joy at how gas was free that day.

With this newfound information, not only did I feel hopeless, but I even started questioning out loud if it was wise of us to come on the trip in the first place. I immediately forgot all the joy, memories, and intentional time that had happened between me and beautiful Sarahbeth, and all I could see was the problem before me. To make matters worse, we were closer to being in the red than ever, and we were closer to the last paycheck than we were to the next one. It may not sound like much, but when you've been in that situation, it feels like you're in a hole you can't get out of and it's only getting deeper by the second.

Eventually, I had run out of negative remarks to make, and I just sat in my seat in silence. The bad news was the worry had now become full on anxiety. The good news, I was finally done talking so now Jesus had room to start. I started thinking of the sheep in the field that day during one of our many stops. They were perfectly content. Even in the midst of us screaming random animal noises at them. It wasn't until they heard the voice of their shepherd that they moved. Funny enough, they didn't seem to worry at all about two strangers in the field, nor did they seem to worry about much of anything. They grazed in the field until their shepherd called to them. Then, they got up from the ground and ran to eat the food he had brought. It reminded me of my Shepherd.

I felt a soft hand slowly sliding into mine as I heard the words of my bride. "Let's just pray. 'Jesus, we forgot to turn off the pump. We're sorry for our mistake. We ask that you would return to us all that we lost. In your name we pray Jesus, amen." As soon as the prayer had ended, I knew that was all we could do. I did my best to act like one of the sheep who ignored my strange noises every time I thought of the gas pump. Before I knew it, I was waking up to our plane rolling onto the tarmac and the attendant overhead welcoming us home to DFW International Airport. Upon arrival I opened my phone and touched the little plane icon to restore service to my device. Pretty quickly, the notifications were rolling in. At the top of the list was one from our banking app. I thought I was dreaming when I read the words that the direct deposit was available.

"Sarahbeth what is this?" I asked, grabbing her attention. We both stared at the number with a puzzled look. We had received a direct deposit for a sum that was almost the exact amount that we had lost to our unmet RV friends. I clicked on the alert and began to investigate. There was no name associated with the deposit. There was only an account number we didn't recognize. I called the bank the next morning and they didn't have answers. All they knew was the deposit was real and that was the end of it. We never heard from anyone and the more we tried to find answers, the more questions we had. Maybe our Icelandic gas station returned us the money or maybe it was an error by the bank, but perhaps it was our Shepherd coming to the field and calling out to us. Maybe He was helping us turn off the pump. All I know is, when you choose to live by faith, coincidence no longer exists.

We had been returned the full amount we had lost and then some. I closed my eyes and began to thank Jesus. An international plane ride earlier we were asking the Lord to return what was lost, and eleven hours later it arrived. All that worry and in the end it would all work out. When worry comes knocking on your door, it normally forgets to inform you that if you just wait on your Shepherd, it will all work out.

I think a lot of us tend to forget to turn off the pump. We fill our minds and hearts with the cares of this life and let worry lead us to irrational places. We start to dream in the negative and before you know it, we forget about rule number two. Jesus had the same rule. In Matthew 6:25-26, He is telling His disciples all about rule number two. He explains it like this:

> *Therefore I say to you,* **do not worry about your life**, *what you will eat or what you will drink; nor about your body, what you will put on. Is not life more than food and the body more than clothing? Look at the birds of the air, for they neither sow nor reap nor gather into barns; yet your heavenly Father feeds them.* **Are you not of more value than they?** *Emphasis added.*

In other words, He is saying to His followers "*Hey! If you are going to follow me, then this is a worry-free zone!*" It isn't that you can't have hard days and moments of uncertainty. Come on, this is life were talking about, it seems as though nothing ever goes according to plan. However, believers that believe know that He is big enough to work it all out, even when we forget to turn off the pump. It's not about never having cares in this life, it's about what you do with them when they come. I don't know what worries you have or how you came to get them. I do know that sometimes the pump we forget to turn off the most is the one in our mind; the one that keeps flowing in with more and more stress and worry until it becomes full on anxiety.

My friend Peter has some pretty good advice on how to turn off the pump! He says it like this in chapter 5, verse 7 of his book, 1 Peter:

> *Cast all your cares upon **Him**, for **He** cares for you. Emphasis added.*

"Him" in this verse is Jesus. A really big Jesus who can carry what we can't, and He does it because He cares for you. I think that's what happens when we forget to turn off the pump, we make it about our cares and not His, and His care is for you and for me. We were never created to carry worry, and when we dream, it isn't supposed to be negative. It's supposed to be like rule number two. Jesus is big enough to carry all of our worry and He loves to work it all out in the end. We just get to be like those sheep in the field that don't move until our Shepherd comes to meet us. Just look at the birds, they aren't worrying! So why should you? The birds know that He is a really big Jesus, and He cares for them. How much more for you! At least those are the words of a really big Jesus. Next time worry comes knocking on your door and you feel the cares of this life coming like thorns, try rule number two and give it to a big Jesus, even if it's your own fault because you've forgotten to turn off the pump.

"Jesus, thank you that YOU are my good shepherd who cares for me! Would you destroy any box I have made around how you will take care of me, and would you give me the faith to stop worrying? Jesus, help me cast all my cares upon you!"

Chapter 4

FORD EXPLORER

Provision for what I need is Jesus' responsibility!

One thing I've learned about Jesus is that He loves to show us His character—especially when there is something we've yet to really grasp and understand about Him. You can normally tell when you fall into this category because you stop living by rule number two from the previous chapter. It's like when you know scripture tells you God is a provider and so all seems good, until you forget to turn off the pump and unforeseen expenses come your way. You quickly forget what scripture said. Ever been there? Whenever rule number two goes out the window, it only exposes that you don't know how big Jesus is, and there is something about His character you just don't quite understand yet. Jesus sees these moments as opportunities to play peek-a-boo and show Himself to you in a new way. When sweet little Rosie hit the three-month mark, she started being able to comprehend when she was alone. It was the cutest thing to hide yourself behind your own hands and watch as she processed that the person who was right in front of her had just left. Then, right before she started to breakdown and cry you could remove your hands exposing your face and shout "PEEK-A-BOO!" Sweet little Rosie would start to giggle, and she would come to realize she wasn't alone. We'd play this for several minutes until she finally understood it was a game and I actually wasn't going anywhere.

I think Jesus does the same with us when life throws circumstances our way that we didn't expect. We often lose sight of Jesus, and then we begin to amplify all that's going on around us. Eventually, we start to forget He is with us and how big He really is. In these moments, when our many circumstances start to become bigger in our mind than He is, we can sometimes breakdown and lose it too. All too often, right before the tears start to flow, here He comes ready to show His face. This normally happens over and over until we finally realize He isn't going anywhere. He is here to stay. The point of peek-a-boo Jesus is for us to come to an understanding in our hearts and fully grasp who He is and what He is like.

In 1 Corinthians 10:3-4, Paul writes this:

> *For though we walk in the flesh, we do not war according to the flesh. For the weapons of our warfare are not carnal but mighty in God for pulling down* **strongholds**.

Now, in verse 5, Paul is going to define what a stronghold is. He continues on saying:

> *Casting down arguments and* **every high thing that exalts itself against the knowledge of God**, *bringing every thought into captivity to the obedience of Christ. Emphasis added.*

Paul defines a stronghold as every high thing that exalts itself above the knowledge of God. Maybe you're like me and you are asking, "What does that mean? What is a 'high thing'?" I am not a world class theologian but let me break it down for you. Another translation defines a stronghold as *human reasoning that becomes a proud obstacle that keeps you from knowing who God is.* Simply put, it's our own fears and worries that we make bigger than Jesus. Any circumstance or issue in our lives that becomes bigger than Him is a high thing. We often construct our own human reasoning and try to figure out what to do, but maybe Jesus just wants to play peek-a-boo and show you His face. Religion tells us we pull down strongholds by having more faith. Muster it up. *"Come on, stir up your faith people, you should know better!"* You know, that kind of thing. Believers who believe just look to Jesus. They take scripture at its word and cling to the truth of who Jesus is no matter what comes their way. He is far too big to be dethroned and no high thing can get above Him. Not a political mindset or a religious tradition. Not circumstance nor issue. Not even our own human reasonings.

Upon returning from our trip to Iceland, we went back to life as usual. Beautiful Sarahbeth and I both returned to our jobs and our financial world was back to its normal balance. That normal balance, however, had yet to come to an understanding and fully grasp who Jesus is as our provider, and He was getting ready to play peek-a-boo with me. If anything had been exposed in my life in the previous twenty-four hours, it was the fact that I had been living under the belief that I was my own provider and even more so that I was the provider of my family. All was good as long as I was in control. This is a pretty normal mindset of human reasoning in the world. If you're a man, then that means you provide for your family. You work long hours or two jobs if you have to, but it's your responsibility to pay the bills and make sure all the needs of the family are met. It's really heroic and sweet. The problem is, human reasoning is a lot of pressure to take on, and it teaches people to look to men as their provider instead of looking to Jesus. In the previous chapter, we looked at Matthew 6 and how Jesus explains rule number two. But let's look again at verse 26.

> *Look at the birds of the air, for they neither sow nor reap nor gather into barns; yet your **heavenly Father** feeds them. Are you not of more value than they?*

Who does it say feeds them? In case you have a hard time with the answer, it's the two words in bold. Our Heavenly Father. Notice it doesn't say our earthly father feeds us. Oh no. It is very specific to let us know provision comes from our heavenly Father. Here is another one from Philippians 4:9 to help drive home this point.

> *And **my God** shall supply all your need according to His riches in glory by Christ Jesus. Emphases added.*

Let me ask you again, who is it that supplies all our need? The answer, again, is in bold. If there is a need you have, it's Him who wants to supply it. As I have searched scripture, I have found one particularly liberating truth: God never asked me to be a provider, that's His job. So consequently, I have had to learn to not be the hero and let that be Jesus. However, I am getting ahead of myself. Back to our return from Iceland where I have just recovered from the gas pump that almost took me out.

About a week back into our normal swing of things, we found ourselves on date night. Side note: Thursdays are date night. Every Thursday, regardless of rain or shine, beautiful Sarahbeth and I go on a date. Even though we've said "I do," we still date each other. It keeps things fresh and the romance alive. On this specific date night, as we sat at dinner, I asked if there was anything new my sweet bride felt like the Lord was speaking to her. In fact, there was.

"I know it doesn't make sense, but I feel like the Lord is asking me to step away from my job and not work for a while." She said with curious uncertainty.

"How long is a while?" I quickly responded, with a tone that implied I was questioning what was just said. She went on to explain that for the next six months, she felt like she was not supposed to work and instead dedicate her time to prayer and seeking the Lord. She also wanted to spend more time learning new skills like playing the piano and growing in leadership.

Six months was a long time and that would require us to adjust from two incomes to one. I passive aggressively tried to reason her out of the idea and state the facts. The facts were, we had bills to pay. Not only did we have living expenses, but a car loan as well. We were comfortably living on two incomes, and I was happy that way. Living on one income would require faith that I was unsure I had, and it would force me out of control and into looking at Jesus to supply all our needs. We decided we would "pray about it" and not make any quick decisions. Praying about it is good, so don't hear me wrong, we must always be in prayer about all things. That's the way you live your life when you're a believer who believes. However, "I'll pray about it" can often be a safe phrase to communicate "I don't want to deal with this right now", and Jesus can see right through that. The truth is, I was unsure if I had the faith to do something like that. It would force me to put my money where my mouth was. Quite literally. It would also mean surrendering control of what I thought I was in charge of, but that was the first step to crushing this box labeled "finances".

Beautiful Sarahbeth made me a man of my word and that evening we were praying about it together. Again, we would only pray a simple prayer—nothing profound or eloquent. If I remember correctly, it probably sounded something like this: *"Lord, if this is you, would you put a conviction in us to take a step of faith; a conviction we can't shake."*

Well, we weren't able to shake it, and about a month later we were down to one income. I would like to tell you that it was an easy decision, and it was another one of those experiences where a super jacked angel came and told us what to do. You know, the angel with muscles the size of my head. However, that wasn't how it played out. I was terrified of the decision, but my bride had the conviction that it was time for a step of faith. That step felt more like a jump, but we did it together. The first week felt more like a rush of adrenaline than anything, but pretty soon reality set in and our mailbox became full of those little white envelopes that read "statement enclosed." It was time to pay the bills.

At our wedding, beautiful Sarahbeth's granddad shared a toast in which he let me know that one thing I must always remember to tell my new wife is this phrase: "Honey, the bills are paid!" and so far, I was a hundred percent for saying that phrase every month, but I wasn't going to be able to say that this month. We had more bills to pay than money in the bank, and I was scratching my head unsure of what we were going to do.

However, that weekend, as I was leaving our church, the finance director approached me with a peculiar question. "Aaron, are you expecting some money to come in?" I was caught off guard and was confused on how he knew what we were going through.

"What do you mean?" I guardedly replied.

He handed me an envelope that had my name on it and started to explain. "This was in the offering box. It's addressed to you specifically by name. I don't know who it's from and it doesn't say why. So, I was wondering if you were expecting money. Anyways it's yours."

I wasn't expecting money, Jesus was playing peek-a-boo and He had my attention. In the envelope was the exact amount we needed for me to look across the table and say "Honey, the bills are paid!" All of a sudden, I had faith for this step, too.

With one month down, we had five more to go. I didn't know how God was going to do it, but I knew He was teaching me something about who He is. And who He is, is a Provider. But again, I was used to being in control with the finances, and when that's all you know, it's how you operate. I started going into military mode with what we spent and informed beautiful Sarahbeth she needed to run every expense by me before making it. It was my attempt at being our provider. Even when Jesus was trying to take on those responsibilities, I was clinging on where I could. That's what happens when you use human reasoning. The more I tried to control, the more I would think about Philippians 4. *"My God shall supply all your needs."* Eventually, I surrendered that control and told beautiful Sarahbeth that if it was a need, she could swipe away. No discussions were needed, and no questions would be asked. "Needs" fell under Jesus' responsibilities. Not mine. Not hers. It was uncomfortable and confronting, but smashing boxes always feels that way.

One evening, I was coming home from a long day at work when we received an invitation to go to dinner with a couple that we deeply admire. We cleared our schedule and headed straight there. When money is tight, and you're invited to a free dinner, you go. That's newlywed 101. We met at a mom-and-pop pizza joint that used lava lamps as their theme for decoration. Upon entering the restaurant, we were greeted with a whiff of fresh mozzarella and rosemary olive oil baked bread, while Elton John was playing overhead. It's safe to say it was a vibe. The four of us sat down and we enjoyed the evening admiring the restaurant and catching up on all that life had brought our way. As we transitioned from our thin crust entree and into our chocolatey based dessert, the husband put both of his elbows on the table and leaned in closer than he had previously.

"There was a reason we asked the two of you to meet us for dinner this evening. We wanted to talk about your family!"

Up until this point, we had avoided the topic of finances and had not made this amazing family aware of our current situation. We also weren't pregnant and had no plans in the near future to conceive. So, hearing talk about "family" was interesting to us. We leaned in to eagerly hear what was next.

"Sooner or later the two of you will begin to have kids. First, you'll have one and then not long after, I'm sure more will follow.

We've been praying for you guys, and we felt the Lord leading us to bless your family."

"Wow. Thank you." I replied, not knowing for sure how they intended to bless us. "Wow" is a word we use when we are acknowledging what someone is saying but don't quite know how to respond. I am not sure where "wow" originated from, but if you ask me, I think someone was without words and just shouted out, "WOW." That's what it stands for, right? With Out Words? Anyways, I am rabbit trailing. After my without words moment, the husband continued.

"If it's okay with you guys, we would like to buy you a car. Something that could be a family vehicle."

My without words moment was growing, but before I could even search for the words to respond, the man continued.

"We'd like you to pick out the car that you want. You can go to any dealership of your choice and test drive the cars you're deciding between, and when you've made your choice, we will come purchase it in your name. And how about this, let's stick to a budget of $50,000."

Immediately I thought the pizza I had just consumed was going to make a second appearance. I didn't have any of my beverage in my mouth, but if I had, it would've been sprayed all over the table and onto the couple by the shock that felt like a punch in the gut. I mean, what do you do when you hear something like that? Do you play it cool and act like $50,000 is a normal amount of money to just give away at a dinner table? Do you break down in tears, saying thank you? Maybe you shout and act like you've just hit the jackpot in Vegas. I don't know the correct way to respond, but I am pretty sure I looked like a deer caught in headlights. Now it was my facial expression that was saying "wow". The whole interaction, beautiful Sarahbeth was squeezing my hand under the table as tight as she could, and I am pretty sure tears filled our eyes as the words flowed from his lips.

"We do have one condition." The husband inserted. I quickly began to think maybe all this was too good to be true as I felt my guard start to rise. I was so confused thinking about what it possibly was that they could want from us. Little did I know, all of this was the buildup to the peek-a-boo moment where Jesus was getting ready to show us His face.

"And here it is," He continued. "Whenever someone asks you about the car, you tell them that God bought it for you. Don't ever mention our names. We are doing this because we felt the Lord asking us to bless you. It's Him."

And there it was, peek-a-boo! Jesus was showing us who He is, and who He is, is a big ole provider. Not only did the couple buy us the car, but we sold the one we owned and used the money to pay off all our debt. We were making less money than we ever had, yet somehow, we had more than we ever imagined. Not only was every need met, but not once did we come close to going without. The whole time, He proved to us that He is our provider - not me, not beautiful Sarahbeth, and not our two incomes. Our provider is Him and Him alone.

The Bible is very clear; needs are His responsibility. That's the thing with His leadership, if you jump when He says jump, then you'll find that He catches you. He provided a sacrifice for Abraham, water from a rock in the wilderness, and manna from

Heaven for the children of Israel. He provided a leader when Israel needed one. He provided a coin from a fish's mouth, and He provided a sacrifice that would redeem and forever atone the sin of the world. He provides for the lilies and the roses of the fields, He even does it for the birds in the sky and the swimming creatures in the sea, even the weird scary ones. Yet how much more will He surely provide for you and me. He does all this because needs are His responsibility! Not yours, not mine, they are His!

After that six-month period, we were debt free and living with a new conviction: Jesus is the provider for our family, and He has a really big pocketbook. Before leaving her job, beautiful Sarahbeth didn't have the ability to play the piano. Today, I come home to find her sitting at her ivory upright playing away and growing in the skills she learned during that time away from her job. Shortly after the time frame of six months that she felt like the Lord had given, she was offered a new job. One where she could grow in leadership and exercise the call of God on her life. I stopped trying to put man's reasoning around what it looks like to be financially stable or successful. I let go of control and let needs fall off my shoulders and onto His. It hasn't been easy, but then again, faith never is. However, it has been full of Jesus showing up in strange ways, like envelopes in the offering box and random dinners at lava lamp pizza joints.

From time to time, we still have to grab hands under the table and remind ourselves that needs are His responsibility and not ours. Every once in a while, there is an unforeseen expense that reveals where I again am attempting to regain control and take on the pressure of being the provider of our family. Sometimes we feel the temptation to let money be emotional and overwhelm us a little too much. But every time things don't make sense, or we are waiting on a need to be filled, we go outside and say, "Wow," as we look at our Ford Explorer - the one that God bought for us. Sometimes we take it for a spin around the block and talk about all the strange ways He has shown us who He is and what He is like. It never fails that the Ford Explorer always reminds us of how big Jesus is and in what big ways He always provides for us.

"Jesus, thank you that YOU are my provider! Today, I lay down the pressure of providing for myself and I declare that you are big enough to supply all of my needs. Would you destroy any boxes I've made around your provision and give me the faith to trust you with my finances!?"

Chapter 5

HELLO, MY NAME IS JESÚS

…and I'll be taking care of you today!

Every year for July Fourth, our church staff takes the entire week off. We put everything on hold, and we spend the entire week with family and friends celebrating Independence Day and enjoying the summer sun. I should probably say that most things get put on hold. If you work for a church, you'll know exactly what I mean, especially if you're on administrative staff. We all go our separate ways and do different things. Some travel. Some take the week and binge the newest show. Some take some much need R & R. For me and beautiful Sarahbeth, we normally go stay with my parents in their small and quiet West Texas town. It's very low key. When you live in the heart of a metroplex like ours, low key always sounds nice. In the summer of 2019, however, we decided to switch it up a bit. Just a few weeks before the fourth, I was fast at work in my office when I heard a knock on the door frame. It was Tony. Tony was new to the staff and had just taken a role as the new finance guy. He is brilliant at what he does, but that's not what makes him special. Tony has one of the purest hearts you'll ever know, and he is always looking to make a new friend in a memorable way. Tony and his amazing wife, Alba, were going to spend the break week in Tulum, Mexico, and he stopped by my communal office to see if we wanted to tag along. Tony offered to work it out in our budget and promised it would be a good time. When the finance guy comes to you and offers to work a beach trip into your budget, you say yes. It's like having a free consultant. Within the week, Tony had booked us roundtrip flights and snagged us an Airbnb in the jungle of Tulum. It all came together so fast and with so much ease that it seemed as if it was a table that was prepared for us, and all we had to do was sit down. Before you knew it, the fourth had arrived, and we were driving down the Mexican highways to our vacation paradise.

Tulum is known for its beautiful, secluded beaches and well-preserved ruins of an ancient Mayan port city. It sits on the Caribbean coastline of Mexico's Yucatán Peninsula. Scattered around the region are freshwater cenotes. Cenotes, (pronounced Sea-No-Tays), are water filled sinkholes that have naturally occurred in limestone rock when an underground cave collapses on itself and exposes the groundwater. They are heavy tourist attractions and filled with some of the most refreshing water in the world. They are as clear as glass and you can see every underwater creature swimming around that's made its home in that cenote. If that isn't enough, just a couple hour drive from Tulum is one of the seven wonders of the world. The great Chichén Itzá. It is a massive pyramid created by the ancient Mayans. Just standing at the foot of this hundred-foot stone mountain is truly breathtaking. It really makes you wonder.

Tulum had become a popular destination across our community in Dallas and we had several friends who had made the trip before, so we decided to ask them for their best recommendations. There were many things that could've received a high Yelp review, but across the board the most common answer was a beach spot named *Hartwood*. An off-grid, open-air restaurant known for its seafood cooked over a wood-burning grill. All the fish would be deep sea caught that day and prepared before guests would arrive. It was surrounded by the jungle and just off the mouth of the shoreline.

"If you're going to eat there, you need to make sure you get a reservation. Otherwise, you won't get in." That was the most common phrase we heard when discussion of Hartwood would come up. It was at the top of our list of places to go.

Upon arrival to the stunning town of Tulum, we checked into our Mayan home and headed straight for the beach. On the way there, we made sure to give the hostess at *Hartwood* a call. The phone rang for about five minutes before we decided to hang up and try again later. At the beach, we found a beautiful spot under a canopy and spent the afternoon soaking up the sun and enjoying the salty water. Sarahbeth had an idea to open the scriptures and read a psalm on the sand. We flipped over to the twenty-third one and read it out loud to each other. Verse 5 seemed to be one that jumped out at us that day, and we spent the latter portion of our beach day discussing it.

You prepare a table before me in the presence of my enemies; You anoint my head with oil.

We had this thought: If Jesus prepares tables for us, what do they look like in our lives? Are they literal tables or is this symbolism to describe how Jesus is with us in the most intense of times? We discussed all the different possibilities that prepared tables could be. Like, perhaps a table could be wisdom from a mother or father during difficult situations. Or possibly it's envelopes that get left for you in the offering box in the middle of hard financial times. We even talked about how this trip felt like a prepared table; in the middle of a crazy metroplex lifestyle, here we found ourselves sitting on the beach talking about Jesus. What a beautiful place to be. What an amazing table to sit at. We laughed as we wondered if Jesus would be the waiter at this prepared table or if it would be that super jacked angel with muscles the size of our head. We decide it would probably be the angel as Jesus would most likely be sitting with us.

After leaving the beach, we decided to explore one of the nearby cenotes and get the full Tulum experience. On the way, we picked up the phone to seal our Hartwood reservations.

"It's just ringing. No one is picking up." Tony shared as he patiently waited to talk to someone on the other end of the line. We eventually gave up and decided we would attempt again at another time. We all enjoyed the cenote, and after a long day, we decided to do a light dinner and get some rest. That next morning, as we started our day, we finally made it through to the hostess at the open-air restaurant.

"Unfortunately, we don't have any open reservations through the end of the week. How about a time next week?" They were completely booked. Our friends weren't kidding when they said this restaurant was the best. There wasn't a single availability throughout our entire time there. We would be leaving in three days, so next week wouldn't work. We tried to explain our situation to the hostess through the phone. She politely informed us that there was nothing she could do. She welcomed us to come and wait outside of the restaurant to see if there was a cancelation or a reservation that was a no-show, before hanging up the phone. We were bummed. The four of us are all foodies so we definitely were watering at the mouth every time we thought of the wood-burning grilled fish. But instead of letting us get ourselves down, we decided to go wait it out at the restaurant and try to get in. Why not? We thought again about verse 5 of Psalm 23. *"He prepares a table for us."* Maybe there would be one prepared for us here, right next to the open flame grill, where we could watch them cook the freshly caught fish. Later that day, after we cleaned up from a long day swimming in the sun, we headed to the restaurant. It was still early in the evening, and we thought we could try to beat the rush. Upon arriving, we couldn't even find a parking spot. The entire strip along the beach was lined with cars bumper to bumper. So much for trying to beat the rush. We drove around in circles for about thirty minutes before we finally found a car that was leaving their spot. We immediately jumped on it and started walking to the front desk to see if something awesome would happen.

As we approached the restaurant, we saw the hostess booth under the white and black painted Hartwood sign. There was a party of four standing at the booth and several other similar sized groups waiting to be seated for their reservations. We jumped in line behind the group of four and waited for it to be our turn to put our name in. We all questioned if it was even worth a try to get in, but after all the effort of finding that parking spot, we thought we better at least try. That's the thing I have found about traveling with other couples. The key to having a memorable time is going with people who are in to "try." It makes things exciting and leaves room for unexpected moments.

That's what we loved about being in Tulum with Tony and Alba. At any given moment, to try something new, we would look at each other and say these words: "I'm down." Saying "I'm down" is like saying *I'm in*, or *I'll join, I'll do it*. It's not being afraid or scared of being told no. Someone who is down is in for the cause or willing to take the risk. For those of you who are having a hard time catching on, let me give you an example. If I were to ask you if you wanted to go get ice cream and you did, you could respond by saying, "I'm down." I think believers who believe are always *down*. They know that those are the moments that Jesus puts His awesome power on display. They are down to pray for outrageous things, they are down to believe that God is on their side, they are even down to wait in a long line at a booked restaurant and think, *What the heck, maybe we'll have favor and get in.*

The hope that we had favor, however, quickly started to slip away when we heard the party of four that was in front us ask for a table and the host respond.

"We have no openings tonight or through the end of the week. I am so sorry, but unfortunately, we won't be able to get you in." I felt like that was our answer, and I looked at our group with a face that expressed we should probably leave, but we were all still down to try. So after the party of four that was in front us walked away, we stepped up to the hostess.

"Do you have any tables tonight for a party of four? We don't have reservations."

"Unfortunately, we do not. We're all booked. But before you go, let me do this for you. I'll check with one of our waiters," the hostess said, as she walked into the restaurant to ask one of the waiters if there was a table for us. Even at that, we were in shock. I don't know what the difference was between our party of four and the one that was just turned away before us. We watched as she walked over to the back end of the restaurant and began to dialogue with one of the waiters. After about a two-minute conversation, they both nodded their heads and she returned to us at the booth.

"Okay! You're in luck tonight. One of our waiters has an opening and he will be able to serve you. Are you all ready now?" She grabbed four bundles of silverware and motioned her hand towards the inside of the restaurant to direct us. She walked us right past every party that was waiting on their reserved table and through the sitting area to a table in the back. It was positioned right next to kitchen and had a front row seat to the wood-burning grill. You could smell every spice and herb as it sizzled on the fire. We couldn't believe it. We had gotten a table in the midst of many being turned away.

As the hostess sat us at our table, she told us that our waiter would be with us shortly. Just a few minutes later, we saw a young man that looked to be right around thirty years old coming our way. He had dark olive skin and a white apron that expressed he was restaurant staff. He was carrying a large menu made of wood that was about three feet in height. As he approached our group, he set his menu on the edge of the table and smiled at us with an expression that was contagious as he introduced himself.

"Hello, my name is Jesús. I will be taking care of you today. I am so glad we were able to get you in. Our team set this table up by the grill just for you. Before I get your drinks, can I go over our menu for the evening with you?" He said with his Hispanic accent.

He began to explain how all the fish on the menu was fresh-caught that day and what he would recommend.

"I also suggest you get the bread," he continued.

I think the argument from a few days earlier was solved. When the Lord prepares a table for you, it's He who comes to serve you. Not that super-ripped angel. He was probably around here somewhere, but we were too in awe of the fact that our waiter was named Jesus and he had gotten us in. Not only that, but he was feeding us fish and bread. Let me remind you, when you live by faith, coincidence no longer exists. Regardless, if this man was actually our Lord or just a man with the same name was irrelevant. Jesus was speaking to us through this experience that He had a table prepared for us.

Jesús served us that evening with a smile and a welcoming spirit. Each time he would come to our table, he would ask us questions about our trip and lives, and the whole time he was completely engaged with every word we said. At the end of the night, he thanked us for coming in and told us to come back to see him.

I think there are lots of tables in our lives prepared for us that we often don't even realize or see. When you sit at His table, it's

He that takes care of you. Not the other way around. In John chapter 13, Jesus is at the table with His disciples. Here is the account of what happens.

And supper being ended, the devil having already put it into the heart of Judas Iscariot, Simon's son, to betray Him, Jesus, knowing that the Father had given all things into His hands, and that He had come from God and was going to God, rose from supper and laid aside His garments, took a towel and girded Himself. After that, He poured water into a basin and began to wash the disciples' feet, and to wipe them with the towel with which He was girded. Then He came to Simon Peter. And Peter said to Him, "Lord, are You washing my feet?" Jesus answered and said to him, "What I am doing you do not understand now, but you will know after this." Peter said to Him, "You shall never wash my feet!" Jesus answered him, "If I do not wash you, you have no part with Me."

When you're sitting at the table with Jesus, His desire is to serve you. This is a challenging concept for believers because we often attempt to win God's love by serving Him. We think all of our doing will somehow draw us closer to Him or cause us to be loved a little more than we already are, but this just simply is not the gospel. The truth is Jesus came to serve, and He told Peter, if you do not let me do this, then you have no part in me. In other words, He is saying that if you want to be close to Him, sit at His table and let Him serve you. I have a theory. This account in John 13 is just days after Jesus had sent the disciples out in twos to preach the Kingdom. You see the full account in Matthew 10 and in verse 14 Jesus says something powerful.

And whoever will not receive you nor hear your words, when you depart from that house or city, shake off the dust from your feet.

When you aren't received, Jesus says to shake the dust from your feet. My theory is this: just to make sure all the dust was truly shaken from the feet of the disciples, Jesus decided He would help, get down on His knees, and wash them. Even between the toes. He does this at His table. He comes serving you the best fish and bread, and He looks at you with His warm smile and, sometime during the meal, He washes you of every piece of dust you've picked up. I think that's why verse 5 of Psalm 23 says the table is prepared in the presence of your enemies. Just to remind you that even in the middle of it, His desire is to feed you and keep you clean. He even gets down between the toes.

I think every time we are going through something we don't understand or something that seems really challenging, we need to remind ourselves just how big Jesus is. A big Jesus has a really big table. He prepares it just for you, even if it's in the midst of your enemies. He has tables that He prepares for families and marriages. He prepares tables in your workplace and for your friends. There is not a guest list that's exclusive for this table and there is not a limited number of seats. There is a chair that has your name on it and a plate with fresh-caught fish just for you. You are always received at this table, and you will never be left out. Crazy to think, even Judas sat at the table. In the passage of John 13, at the dinner in the upper room, Judas ate the food and drank the wine too. Jesus knew that night that Judas would betray Him, yet even in the midst of it, there was a prepared table with a seat for the betrayer. If it was the case for him, then I know it's true for you and me. Sometimes, when we mess up in our lives or don't quite live up to par in our Christian walk, whatever par even is, we often think we have to work to gain back merit with God and regain our seat at the table, but that's just not the good news of the gospel. The good news of the gospel is that there was a seat for Judas too, even on the night that Jesus was betrayed. That tells me that nothing can remove our seat from this table. Nothing will keep Jesus from preparing your spot. Even when it seems as if the restaurant is full and there are no more reservations for the week. Maybe you've lived your life at this table, or maybe you feel like there has never been a spot prepared for you. Maybe, just maybe, if you are bold enough to be *down* and ask the Lord if there is an open table for you and your friends, you might just hear a beautiful response in the midst of all the craziness of your life.

"*Hello, my name is Jesús. I will be taking care of you today!*" I bet He will even wash your feet and get in-between the toes.

"Jesus, thank you for preparing a table for me. Would you break any boxes I have around how you serve me at your table? You have a seat just for me and it's here where you wash my feet from the dust I've picked up along the way. Give me the faith to see you today and this table YOU have prepared for me!"

Chapter 6

WIN OR LOSE

Jesus and all of Heaven are cheering for you!

I haven't told you much about myself or my upbringing up until this point. That's not really the point of these pages! The point is to see Jesus bigger than we ever have before. However, to really articulate just how big Jesus is, and has been, to me, I want to take you back to the beginning. All the way back to 2001, when I was just getting ready to enter into the second grade. At that time, my family lived in a single-family home with a green roof that sat across the street from a small park. We would go as a family of four and swing in the evening and watch as the West Texas sunset would hit the horizon. I have one sibling who is absolutely stunning at almost everything she does. I call her E. E is just about two-and-half years older than me, so growing up we were always close and would go on adventures together. She was my big sister and my role model. Our parents met in church and that's exactly where they planned to raise us - in a Southern Gospel Pentecostal church that was at the center of our small country town. As a family, I remember anytime the church doors were open, we were all there. My dad was on the elder board and my grandparents would lead worship. I'll never forget how, when service seemed to be exceptionally powerful, my grandma would throw her head back and let loose on the keys. I would look over and see my uncle shredding on the guitar and Grandpa singing praises to the Lord. We would sing songs like "I Sing Praises to Your Name" and "Days of Elijah." It was a family affair! Even E and I would often get up after the main worship time and sing a special. A special was a song where someone from the congregation would sing a solo or a duet to the church before the sermon. We would do dinner every evening together at 5:00 p.m., and afterwards, we would do a devotional or read a part of scripture together. It was true of our home that we served the Lord. It wasn't just a part of our lives that we fit in each week or a set of values to live by. Church and the Bible was normal life in the Smith home. The only thing that was missing, was a big Jesus.

In the summer just before I would go into the second grade, a day came that I would remember forever. I still remember playing with Legos on the floor of my bedroom with the bunkbeds, when my dad came and told me to come into the living room. I passed by the only bathroom in the house as I saw my mom doing her hair with the pink rollers. E came out of her room, and we joined each other on the couch. We were sitting underneath the massive family portrait, (the one that had a white scuff on Mom's eye from where we had been playing football in the house.) We were used to having family talks, but this time there was a sense of seriousness in the atmosphere that I wasn't familiar with. I still remember it being in the morning on a sunny day when Dad got down on his knee in front of us. Mom came out of the bathroom and stood in the entrance of the hallway next to the living room. As our dad began to open his mouth, tears started to fill his eyes. His voice got a little shaky as he said the words.

"Things are going to start looking a little different around here. Your mother and I have decided to get a divorce."

As a second-grader, you can't even spell divorce. So I had no idea what was being said in the moment, but I knew it wasn't good by the way E began to cry and ask why. I couldn't tell you anything else about that day. I couldn't tell you how I responded or where the family talk went from there. I just know that day felt like a gut punch, and it would take more than a decade to catch my breath.

Over the coming weeks, E and I would pack up the things in our bedrooms and move them into boxes. We said goodbye to our friends in the neighborhood and to the park across the street. The two of us would load our things into the back of that old extended cab two-tone pickup truck and leave that house with the green roof behind. E and I would move with our mom into an apartment complex called Adobe Creek. Room number 28. The only positive thing about it was that there was a staircase to the part of the apartment where my new room was. I couldn't break it down to my friends or explain what was happening to my teachers at school. All I knew was something very wrong had hit our home. I unknowingly put a sticky note on my heart that day. Sticky notes on our hearts are like systems of beliefs we live under that are created by the circumstances we experience. It's like an internal vow you subconsciously make that effects the way you live moving forward. These sticky notes can say all sorts of different things, for instance, my sticky note from that day said: *If you follow God and serve in His house, then you'll end up with a broken home.* I didn't know if I still believed in God, but if I did, I hated Him. How could He let this happen to our family?

We continued going to church, but when E and I were with Mom, we would attend a new one that we had never been to before. At this new church, they had a youth group where the teenagers would gather and play games and have worship that sounded like radio songs. Sometimes the youth pastor would let me come with E and I thought about how this place seemed really cool. However, I didn't think the same about God. How could I? I blamed Him for the reason I was living with only one parent.

Over the next ten years I would learn how to play church. In the building, you behave and put on a smile and act like all is well back at home. But then once you leave, so does the smile. Once I entered into high school, I was a hypocritical pro. On the outside, life was great, but on the inside, I was all tangled up. We had moved churches a couple other times, trying to find breakthrough for our family, but to me, they were all the same. And with each one, that sticky note on my heart just got larger and larger. I developed a pretty significant relationship with sin. In fact, I could probably write a book called *BIG SIN* on all that I got wrapped up in. I was even arrested on one occasion just after my eighteenth birthday. It was a double life at its finest, that was close to leaking out of the secret and being public. There seemed to be no outlet to take all that I was wrestling with, but I did find one space where I felt like I could escape the toxic world on the inside, and it was running.

My freshmen year, I went out for the cross-country team, and there was something about running long distances that seemed to liberate my mind and heart space and give me a break from the internal world that had me bound. Pretty quickly I learned something about myself I didn't know. I was a really good runner. What started as an outlet to take my mind off all I was carrying turned into three trips to the state cross country meet and several collegiate schools interested in giving me a scholarship to come and run. I began to work my entire high school career to get a scholarship to run somewhere. Somewhere other than home. I knew that could be my ticket out of my small town and into something that was larger than me. However, at our state meet my senior year, we didn't compete as well as we'd hoped, and I did not place individually. There was still some interest from colleges, but I hadn't solidified a scholarship. After talking to a scout from Dallas, he recommended I see what I could do at the end of the year during the track season. So I went out for the team and completed in the mile and the two mile races. I did pretty well, but it would all come to a culmination at the district track meet of my senior year—not just my running career, but truly the entire last decade of my life.

E had given her life to Jesus a few years back and started leading worship in the youth ministry and eventually the larger adult services. Pretty quickly she knew she wanted to give her life to worship, and soon after, she would move to Dallas, Texas to attend a Bible school. At the time, we had one family laptop that we all shared. The only real thing we used it for was iTunes. Back then, there was no iCloud or online downloading, but instead, you would physically plug your iPod into the computer and sync all your music onto the device. E would come home from school and download all the latest worship albums and songs to our computer so that she could move them over to her personal devices to take back to school. I would then go in after her and uncheck all of the songs that had to do with praise or worship from the sync list. I would hop on websites like LimeWire and download the latest hip hop or RnB tracks for my devices, making sure that no worship was carried over. This was the normal flow for music downloading.

The night before the district track meet, I decided I would download any new music in the morning before I would leave to get on the school charter bus. Waiting to do something the next morning is always a bad idea. I woke up to an alarm clock that had been ringing for far too long as I realized I had overslept. I jumped out of bed and threw on clothes as I rushed to get out the door. Just before I left, I grabbed my laptop and iPod and connected the two. I fired up iTunes and hit the button that was marked "Sync all." I didn't filter through the genres or follow normal protocol. I just dumped everything onto my device. A grand mix of my latest hip hop downloads and E's worship albums. I headed out the door and made it just in time to catch the bus. The drive was about thirty minutes to our rival's six-lane track where the district meet would take place. The day was one of those where the weather is just plain bad. A cold front had just blown in, and even though it was May in North Texas, it felt like it was a winter day. It was cold and windy. Not many people would show up to watch the races that day due to the weather, and for everyone that had to be there, it was pretty miserable. My race was the mile run. Four laps at almost a sprint's pace. The downside to the mile run is it is at the end of the meet. It is the second to last race, so those that are competing in that run have to wait all day for their event. You spend the day napping on the bus, staying hydrated, and regularly stretching throughout the day. About an hour before your race, you start to warm up. For me, I started warm up the same way every time: by inserting my headphones and clicking play on my iPod Touch. Music would begin to fill my headspace, and I would begin to prepare for the run.

This specific time, however, was different. I always had the shuffle icon clicked to keep the next play fresh, but because I had dumped the entire library onto my device, there were a lot of songs coming on I didn't know or care for. I think I hit the next button more times that day than I had combined in my whole life. Finally, there was breakthrough, and one of my favorite songs came on that was sure to always hype me up. I would do high knees from the goal line to the twenty-yard line and back. There was about a ten-exercise list I would cycle through as I made my way back and forth across that twenty-yard distance. Once I finished the list, I would move on to a ten-minute jog from end zone to end zone. Just as I launched into my jog, a new song began to ring in my ears. The song was the first track on a live recorded album, so it started out with a crowd cheering. It was an interesting thing. Being in an outdoor stadium with the stands empty but hearing the sound of a screaming crowd in your ears. What I am about to write next is exactly as I remember it.

"*Win or lose today, all of Heaven is cheering for you!*" I remember hearing the words ringing in my heart as the live recorded track played. I was about thirty seconds into my run when I heard the words. It sounded as if it was an audible voice, yet it could only be heard with the internal ears of my heart. I stopped running and took out one of the headphones as I asked myself, *What was that?* Again, I heard the voice in my heart.

"Win or lose today, all of Heaven is cheering for you!" I looked up into the stands and I began to imagine them filled with angels and angelic beings. As I looked, I saw them holding signs with my name, and it seemed as if all of Heaven had shown up that day to watch me run. The lyrics began to come through on the song, and it sounded as if Jesus had walked out of Heaven himself and come to this cold windy track meet to sing me the words.

"Come away with me! It's never too late, it's not too late for you. I have a plan for you, I have a plan for you. It's gonna be wild, it's gonna be great, it's gonna be full of me!" I couldn't explain in the moment what was happening. All I knew was that in a split second, an entire decade caught up with me. I got down on my knees in the middle of 300 teenagers and high school coaches and began to cry. Not the type of cry that can be hidden, either. It was a full out weep. I was encountering the presence of God, and He wanted me to know that He loved me so much that He had come to watch me run.

I had been running from God for years, and it seemed as if in a single moment, He had caught me and these words were healing every wound in my heart that I had picked up as a little kid. He walked right up to my heart and pulled that sticky note off. The one that said: *If you follow God and serve in His house, then you'll end up with a broken home.* He had a plan for me. One that was going to be full of Him. You could make an argument that these were just lyrics to a song, but when Jesus comes to sing over you, it's always different and you never forget it. It's deeper than a melody and it's more than just lyrics. That day on that track, nobody came and prayed for me. Nobody preached the gospel to me or asked me to respond to an alter call. Although, another kid from my school did come over and ask if everything was okay. I just smiled at him and blamed it on allergies. He probably thought I was nuts. Nobody led me in a sinners' prayer, and I didn't need a pastor to tell me what was going on. I gave my life to Jesus that day. I felt a hundred pounds lighter and didn't even realize I had been living life as if I couldn't breathe. Suddenly, it was all fresh air. I couldn't tell you how that day ended or how the race went. I couldn't tell you what I placed or who won the track meet that day. When I think back to that day, all I remember was that was the day that Jesus came to tell me, *"Win or lose, today all of Heaven is cheering for you."'*

David writes in Psalm 95:7-8 about the day of the Lord when His voice comes and says:

> *For He is our God,*
> *And we are the people of His pasture,*
> *And the sheep of His hand.*
> *Today, if you will hear His voice:*
> *"Do not harden your hearts..."*

"Today" had come, and I wasn't about to harden my heart. I had never known about the voice of the Lord. I didn't know that Jesus would speak to us today. Had I known, I probably would've just asked Him why all this nonsense had gone on in my family. I probably would've come to Him and told Him all that I was feeling. At least, that's what I would have liked to believe. The bottom line is, I didn't know His voice because I didn't know Him.

There is another passage in scripture where Jesus is talking about His own voice. He says in John 10:14-16:

> *I am the good shepherd; and I know My sheep, and am known by My own. As the Father knows Me, even so I know the Father; and I lay down My life for the sheep. And other sheep I have which are not of this fold; them also I must bring,* **and they will hear My voice;** *and there will be one flock and one shepherd. Emphasis added.*

Both in this passage and in the one from Psalm 95 we are referred to as sheep that are supposed to hear and know our Shepherd's voice. Remember the story of the sheep in Iceland from chapter 3? Sheep know their shepherd. Even more so, they know their shepherd's voice. It's kind and gentle. It will confront you while simultaneously healing you from a decade of running and deep family pain. It brings life and it directs. His voice does what a thousand others can't. He hadn't been my shepherd and so, by default, I didn't know His voice.

He has this really wonderful thing about His voice. It's so loud, but it comes like a whisper. He never forces it on you, or yells mean words. I think He is actually just waiting for those who will listen. Those who, when "Today" comes, won't harden their hearts. I love the Bible and I love reading all the words that Jesus said. Did you know the most repeated phrase Jesus says in the Bible is this one: "*He who has ears to hear, let him hear!*" If you don't believe me, pull out your phone right now and Google it. I think the main reason God created us with ears is to hear His voice. Here is another one for you. Do you know how faith comes? By hearing!

So then faith comes by hearing, and hearing by the word of God.

Romans 10:17

I love hearing the sounds of nature and animals. I love hearing from loved ones and close friends. I love music and sounds from instruments. But none of these audios compare to the sound of His voice. When you hear His voice, in a moment when faith didn't exist, you're now filled with wonder of who Jesus is and what He is going to do. I believe a really big Jesus has a really loud voice. If you've heard it, you know. You also know it can come like a whisper and that whisper can be heard even when everything else is loud. He doesn't withhold His voice or reserve it for the over-spiritual and most elite. There isn't code you must know to unlock it and you don't even need a paid subscription, you just need ears, and to be honest, they probably don't even need to work. His voice is a part of who He is and what makes Him real.

If you've never heard His voice, just ask Him. You may find Him quick to speak to a decade's worth of pain, or maybe you'll hear Him singing a song over you that you didn't even mean to put on your iPod. Maybe you'll find out that whatever you're going through, He is for you, and you'll hear these profound words that change everything and heal a decade's worth of wounds:

"Win or lose, today all of Heaven is cheering for you!

"Jesus, thank you for your voice. Would you open my ears to hear you today and destroy any boxes I have around how you speak!? I want to know you and I want to know your voice. Would you give me the faith to live on every word YOU speak!?"

Chapter 7

WHEN STORMS ROLL IN

Lean on Jesus, not your own understanding!

In January of 2015, I was starting my last semester of Bible school. I had learned a lot since that cold windy track meet about walking with Jesus. After that day at the track meet, I ended up getting the scholarship I wanted to go run at the collegiate level. However, my life wasn't the same after that day, so I turned it down and instead moved to Dallas, Texas to learn as much as I could about this man named Jesus. Here in Dallas, I became a student in a Bible college where my life would continue to change. I would wake up every morning and walk from the men's dormitories to the track field at the back of the campus and I would spend about an hour every morning walking the four laps that equal a mile, praying. I would pray for all sorts of things as I walked. Things like my future or a spouse. Sometimes I would pray for my grades or for money. I actually probably spent a lot of the time praying for grades and money. When you're a college student, those two things always seem to be right in front of you. Well, they seem to be an immediate need, I mean, because I don't know how much money was in front of me. Not much, but that's beside the point. If I wasn't spending time in prayer, I was sitting in the balcony of the main auditorium reading scripture and trying my best to get a full understanding of it. I specifically liked the Gospels, the first four books of the New Testament. Reading about the life of Jesus from those that walked closest to Him has never gotten old to me. It's actually how I learned all about Him and what He is like. One of my favorite parts is when Jesus had been teaching to the multitudes, and His disciples were so confused, they had to pull Jesus to the side and say: *"Hey Jesus, what are you talking about?"* It was a normal thing for them to not understand the words He was saying. This didn't happen once but on multiple occasions. Here is one example. In Luke 18, Jesus takes His disciples to the side and tells them where they are about to go. He tells them that when they get there, He is going to be brutally murdered. He spells it out for them straight, and this is what the Bible says next:

> *But they understood none of these things; this saying was hidden from them, and they did not know the things which were spoken.*
>
> Luke 18:34

They were scratching their heads and incredibly confused. This is that *"Hey Jesus, what're you talking about?"* moment I mentioned earlier. Those who were the closest to Him normally didn't have understanding of what He was doing. So to follow Him, they would have to surrender their understanding. If it was true for them then, I am sure it's true for us now! I think that's why Jesus tells us to live by faith, because following Him doesn't always make sense. We love talking about the greater and a life filled with Jesus. We don't love laying down our understanding. That's why, instead, we often construct strangely shaped boxes. The wisest book in the Bible, Proverbs, speaks to this in its third chapter.

> *Trust in the Lord with all your heart,*
> **And lean not on your own understanding;**
> *In all your ways acknowledge Him,*
> *And He shall direct your paths. Emphasis added.*
>
> Proverbs 3:5-6

There are actually a lot of places we can healthily lean on in our walk of faith. We can lean on community or mentors in our lives. We can lean on family or friends. We can especially lean on a big Jesus. There are a lot of different places to lean, but when following Jesus, our understanding isn't supposed to be one of them. Not if you're a believer who believes and you are desiring to see the greater. We love the greater, and so did the disciples. Where we get in trouble and create big boxes is when we try to wrap our own understanding around what the greater looks like and how God wants to do it. Ephesians 3:20-21 is a coffee mug favorite. You may even have it framed on the wall in your guest bedroom. My mom would always say it to me when I would go through hard things. It says this:

> *Now to Him who is able to do exceedingly abundantly above all that we ask* **or think**, *according to the power that works in us, to Him be glory in the church by Christ Jesus to all generations, forever and ever. Amen. Emphasis added.*

Exceedingly…abundantly…above all we could ask…**or think!** Think means this: "*You won't be able to understand all that I am going to do.*" Our wildest imagination and greatest frameworks of understanding on our best days wouldn't even come close to who He is and what He is going to do. Like I said, we love that. What we don't love is walking it out before the greater comes. In reading the Gospels, that's what I've found. Those that walked the closest to Him couldn't fit their understanding around what He was doing and saying. They simply had to follow, like sheep.

About a month into my final semester at school, I got a call from one of the teachers. He was well connected across the nation with several churches and pastors, and he wanted me to send over my resume. I would be graduating in just a couple of months, and I knew the next step was to get hired on at a church. I felt in my heart like Jesus had been preparing me to youth pastor. I would be fresh out of school and what better place is there to go take all that I had learned about following Jesus than to a bunch of teenagers? I've been told that if you can preach to teenagers, you can preach to anyone! So I created a resume and sent it over. It was such a bad resume. I had no real leadership experience and had never preached a message in my life. I don't even think I attached a picture of myself. Although, I did have a full heart, a lot of zeal, and a desire to see teenagers meet Jesus! It only took about two weeks before the calls started coming in. I was getting interviews all around the country. I had one in Denver, Colorado, where I could snowboard by day and love on teenagers by night. Maybe I could even snowboard with teenagers and do Bible studies on top of the mountain. I had another interview in San Diego, California. Forget snowboarding. We could do Bible studies on the beach with surfboards and sun tans. There was another one in San Antonio, Texas, where my yearly salary would've been more money than I knew what to do with. There were these and several more in between, so I started the process to see what would happen. All the churches were amazing, with amazing pastors leading the charge. I had no reason to say no to any of them and, in fact, they all would've been an honor to serve at. However, one day when I was out praying around the track, I kept feeling like my stomach was turned upside down every time I thought about saying yes to moving to any of these cities and churches.

"Lord, this doesn't make sense!" I would tell Him as I walked that mile. But I would think about the disciples and about how maybe it wasn't supposed to make sense. It was supposed to be faith. So I did what I thought at the time was the dumbest thing I could possibly do. I called every pastor I had interviewed with and thanked them for the opportunity but respectfully withdrew my resume from the applicant list. Those were the easy conversations. The hard one was the one explaining to the leadership at the school why I had turned down all the opportunities that they had stuck themselves out there to get for me. "*I don't feel like I am suppose to,*" didn't bring a lot of understanding. Not to them or to me. Now I was back to square one, with just under two months from graduating, and I had no idea what was next. Not only that, I felt like I had shot myself in the foot when it came to getting any help from the school. On this side of it, I now know that I was getting nestled perfectly in the position God wanted me so that He could do more than I could ever *think or imagine*!

After a couple months of nothing changing, I was just short of four weeks away from graduation. The thought of that day brought a beautiful mix of excitement and anxiety. Excitement to end one season, and anxiety because I didn't know how I would start the next. E was still living in Dallas and had made her home in the city. She was working downtown and leading worship in a small church right on the border of downtown in the Oaklawn area. On Friday nights, they had late night prayer and worship where about thirty young people would attend for roughly two hours to worship Jesus. I had never been before, but when E invited me, I thought it would be a great space to go and pray about what was to come. Maybe I needed to repent and apologize for turning down the other options, or so the voice of understanding was telling me. Faith was telling me something different. Faith was telling me He was up to something.

The night started with the lights dim and just a few people that had gathered together. The band began to play, and the singers sang as if Jesus was sitting right in the center of the room. The only way to explain the atmosphere is to say you could tell Jesus liked what He was hearing, and He liked it a lot. I had never felt the presence of Jesus quite so strong. I made my way out of my seat and laid on the ground and began to worship Him. A few minutes in, I got out my journal and I am not sure what prompted me, but for some reason I wrote this sentence: *Lord, I want to be in a church just like this.* I quickly prayed that He would speak about what was next for me in life, and I closed my journal and enjoyed the rest of the night. I thanked E for inviting me and went back to my one-bedroom school apartment.

The next week was a normal week for me. Monday through Friday I had school from 8:00 a.m. to noon, and then at 2:00 p.m., I had to be at work. At the time, I was working for an after-school program at a downtown elementary school as a tutor. That Tuesday, while I was at the school, I noticed a massive thunderstorm starting to roll in. The program director encouraged me to take off early and try to beat the storm home. It was one of those storms where the sky gets really dark like it's angry and the wind feels a little personal. Those types of storms where the lightning seems like it has beef with mankind. I ran to my car and within seconds the sky was filled with water, and you couldn't see anything in front of you from out of the windows.

At the time, E was living with a family just a couple blocks from the school, and I called her to ask if I could come ride out the storm at their house. She let the family know, and within a few minutes, I was there in the driveway. I ran up to the door and began to knock. The husband answered the door and welcomed me in. He and his wife were the senior pastors of the church where I had attended the Friday night prayer set.

"Hey I'm Michael. Come in! We're just about to sit down for dinner," He invited me in.

I introduced myself and followed him inside. We sat down at the dinner table and quickly got into one of those conversations that just feels easy. We talked about the school I was attending as well as the elementary school that I worked for. I met their sweet toddler daughters, and they told me all about the church. At some point we got into a discussion about Jesus as I heard about how big He is to their family. I remember thinking that night, *Wow, they really love Jesus.*

Not too long after I arrived, the rain let up and the storm moved on. However, I stayed to have dinner and we talked throughout the evening. Just as dinner was close to ending, Michael asked me a question.

"Aaron, do you know anyone from your school that's getting ready to graduate that's wanting to be in youth ministry? We're currently looking to hire a youth pastor but we just haven't found the right guy!"

"Um…" I paused, caught off guard by the question. That description fit me perfectly, but do you just throw yourself out there and ask for the job? You would probably advise YES! But I got nervous.

"Yeah, I know a lot. I could tell some of them to apply and give them your email?" I proposed. I felt like I again was shooting myself in the foot, but just before the bullet hit my toes, his amazing wife jumped in.

"Michael, Aaron is getting ready to graduate from ministry school!" She just threw it out there, like it was food for thought. Not sure what exactly to say to that, I just timidly responded, "I am…" I felt like sweat was about to start running down the side of my face.

"Okay! Here is my email. Reach out to me this week!" He said as he texted me his information. That next day I sent him an email and by the end of the week I had an interview with the staff for the youth pastor role.

So, just in case you haven't accurately followed the order of events that has just taken place, let me recap. On Friday, I write in my journal: *Lord, I want to be in a church just like this.* The following Tuesday, a storm rolls into town and I end up having dinner at the senior pastor's house. Then, that Friday, exactly a week to the day that I wrote in my journal, an interview for a staff position gets scheduled. You can't make this stuff up. You have to blame that on a big Jesus, one who is up to something!

I had the interview, and long story short, I got the job! I quickly fell in love with the rest of the staff, and they too became like family to me. I wouldn't be graduating with question marks on what was next, and I wouldn't be moving cities. I would be moving downtown. E and I got an apartment together, and over the course of the next several years, this little church would become my big family. I would meet beautiful Sarahbeth a couple of years in, and not too much after, we would get married. Michael would officiate. And then of course, time would bring us sweet little Rosie. That family that opened their home to me on a rainy day would become my family that means the world to me. Those toddler little girls and I would spend many days doing treasure hunts in the backyard and making obstacle courses around the house together. This beautiful family would teach me many things over the years, the biggest being how to love a big Jesus well. All this because a storm rolled in. Exceedingly…abundantly…above all we could ask…**or think!**

Here is another one for you. Isaiah writes in Isaiah 64 what Paul quotes in 1 Corinthians 2:9 (NIV).

> *However, as it is written:*
> *"What no eye has seen,*
> *what no ear has heard,*
> **and what no human mind has conceived"—**
> *the things God has prepared for those who love him.*

The thing is, for God to do what no eye has seen and what no ear has heard also means no human mind can conceive it. That's what a life of faith looks like. Believing in a big Jesus that did, does, and will do what no human mind can conceive.

All this got me thinking, what do we do when storms roll in? And I don't just mean the storms that seem like they have beef with mankind. I think storms roll in all different shapes and sizes. Sometimes they come through family or friends. Sometimes storms roll in like heartache or misfortune. Sometimes the sky gets really dark like it's angry and the wind blowing against you feels a little personal. Storms can be scary and sometimes roll in out of nowhere, but I think storms really mean He's up to something; something exceedingly and abundantly above all we could ask or think. I don't think He sends storms to teach us lessons or humble us. I think storms are just a normal part of the weather forecasts. Although, when storms roll in, I do think He leans over the balcony of Heaven and gathers the angels around Him and says something like, *"Watch me show them how big I am in this storm."* Besides, it was during the middle of a storm that Jesus decided He would walk on water. He performed an act of the greater and did something that we still can't fully understand even to this day, and He did it right in the middle of a storm. Not only that, but He then invited Peter to walk on the water with Him. I'm sure Peter probably felt like the wind was a little personal that day and that he wasn't quite sure how he was going to get out of that one. Yet, just a few moments later, he was walking on the same waves that moments before had scared him. Sure, eventually Peter got nervous and sank into the waves, but Jesus caught him. He had just defied gravity and beat the physics of nature, something his understanding couldn't explain.

Maybe you're in a storm now or maybe you can think back to one that didn't play out the way you hoped. Storms knock down limbs and ruin roofs. The worst of storms can even destroy cities. But maybe in the midst of this storm you're in, or one that a future forecast brings in, you'll find a place to ride out the storm and, just like Peter, you will hear His invitation out of the place of your own understanding and into walking on the waves. Now, for me, whenever storms roll in, I always think: *He must be up to something!*

"Jesus, thank you that you are trustworthy! I don't need to understand you to follow you. Would you break any boxes I have around how you move in my life, and would you give me the faith to trust that even in the midst of the most treacherous storm, your hand is stretched out, inviting me to walk on the water with YOU!?"

Chapter 8

THROWING STONES

Jesus is who He says He is!

They always say the first year of marriage is the hardest. I am not sure who *they* are, but we have all heard of them. *They* say a lot of things. For me and beautiful Sarahbeth, however, what *they* said wasn't true. Our first year was full of adventure, late night pillow talks, and a lot of giggling. That's the way it's supposed to be when you're in love. We made a decision right before we said *I do* that for our first year we weren't going to try and take on the world or find our life rhythm, but instead, we were just going to enjoy one another. Now don't misunderstand me, our marriage isn't perfect, in fact, far from it. In that first year, we still had to work on our marriage and its challenging moments. However, whenever people ask us how our first year was, my answer to this day is always the same. "It was a dream!"

When we talk about our second year, that's not the case. The second year of marriage was extremely challenging for us. We had a lot of conversations with mentors and leaders in our life, asking for advice and seeking counsel. On this side of it, I know that

God was teaching us to overcome together. As individuals, we had both overcome obstacles and hard things before, but as a couple, we hadn't quite found our groove for when challenges came—and let me tell you, a lot would come in our second year. It wasn't that we fell out of love or couldn't get along, it was that we didn't know how to overcome together. It's easy to take on hard things by yourself. There is not another party's feelings or emotions at play. You can "head down and power through" and eventually come out on the other side. When there are two of you, things get interesting. You always want to encourage your spouse to do hard things, but not at the expense of ignoring their heart. You also always want to have empathy, but you don't want to enable them to be a victim to their own situation. Finding the middle takes some practice and you're sure to get it wrong at times. That's when you listen more than you talk and apologize quickly. I am still working on that last part. Anyway, back to the challenges! For starters, it was during this year that Sarahbeth would take six months off from working and we were down to one income. As a team, finding a healthy flow in operating with a budget can be challenging. If you have a spouse, I am sure you know what I am talking about. Until you learn to see it differently, money can always feel emotional, but you've already read about how Jesus was working on us with this one. The big challenge that came that year was called *sciatica*.

The sciatic nerve is the largest nerve in the human body. It begins in your lower back and runs through your glutes and down the back of your thigh, all the way to the sole of your foot. Basically, it affects your entire bottom half. The reason you have a sciatic nerve is to connect the spine to your lower body so that your brain can tell your legs what to do. I am not a doctor, but explaining this to you makes me feel like I should be wearing a lab coat and scrubs. As I continue, you can just imagine me in that attire. *Sciatica* is the term you would use if you experience any pain in your lower back or body that originated from, or is caused by, the sciatic nerve. I hear it's pretty painful and can ruin your day. It usually occurs when someone has a herniated or bulging disc in their spine or a bone spur that presses on the nerve. Once the nerve gets pressed, it sends signals of excruciating pain from your lower back down your entire leg. It can cause the healthiest of people to be completely immobile.

One evening, after we had just crossed into year two of our marriage, we were coming home from dinner. As we left the restaurant and were heading to the car, I notice that my beautiful bride was limping. Now, let me tell you, one of things I learned very quickly about beautiful Sarahbeth is that she is no weakling. Two weeks into us dating we had to go into the ER at the end of one of our dates because she had not one, but five kidney stones. We left the hospital about 2:00 a.m. The next night, my parents came into town, and she was over just before they arrived to meet them with hugs and her big joyful smile. Saying she's tough is an understatement, so to see her limping was not a good sign.

"Honey, are you okay?" I asked her as we arrived at our car.

"My leg just seems so tight! I'm sure I just need to stretch it out." She optimistically replied. We got home and she went to the back room to stretch out and I didn't think much of it. We both love working out and going to the gym. Running for me has always been an outlet to connect with the Lord, and Sarahbeth has an amazing passion for health and fitness. She even works with other women to help them get into a healthy lifestyle. After that night, she would regularly come from her workouts and have stretching sessions in the back room to relieve the pain. The limping also became more regular. Within a couple months she had stopped doing workouts altogether, and the stretches would just make the pain worse. We tried massages and hot baths, but nothing seemed to help or soothe the numbness in her leg. The limping got so intense it started drawing attention, and before we knew it, beautiful Sarahbeth was hurting more than she wasn't. We decided it was time to go see a doctor and get professional help. Some friends had passed along the name of a physician, and we got an appointment booked.

"Tell me, from a scale of one to ten, what would you say the pain is?" The doctor asked upon seeing us.

"Definitely a ten. I can hardly walk most days." Sarahbeth answered in tears. He gave us the lesson on the sciatic nerve and prescribed five weeks of physical therapy. If that didn't work, we would schedule another appointment with this doctor and try another solution. I will spare you the details, but the physical therapy didn't work. In fact, we added to the scale of one to ten and decided it now went up to an eleven. The next step was to get an MRI so we could see exactly what was going on and what was pressing the nerve.

Before I go on with the results of the machine, I think it is important to share these details. We live in a very vibrant community that believes in prayer. In fact, the moment you come around limping, you should just go ahead and wear a T-shirt with a target on it that says, "Come one, come all, I need prayer!" There were many days when we would lay hands on Sarahbeth and pray for her to be healed in the name of Jesus. That's what believers who believe do. They take Jesus at His word and know He is a healer. Especially when you've seen Him do it before. If that's new to you, or if it sounds a little unfamiliar, maybe you should just go head and skip to chapter 9, and then come back to finish this one. However, as time went on, prayer seemed as if it also wasn't working. Every night after dinner we would gather communion and pray, just the two of us. We would thank Jesus for His body that was broken for us and His blood that's stronger than sciatica. We would ask Him to heal my bride's body and believe with all the faith we had that He was going to do it. We would take communion over her body and do it all again the next night. We never turned down prayer, and, in fact, we invited all of it we could get. However, in the midst of all this, we weren't going to pretend like she wasn't in pain. So until a big Jesus healed her, we were going to seek help.

Doctors' offices seem to always feel a little stale. Maybe it's the white walls or the florescent lights but it feels even more stale when you are waiting to hear results. My bride's results were in and the doctor had come to explain them.

"It looks like you have two bulging discs that are squeezing the nerve. That's why it's causing you so much pain and physical therapy didn't seem to work. I am going to be honest, these results are not good," The doctor informed us.

We started asking all the normal questions like what to do and what're our options, but we didn't feel like we were getting anywhere. Finally, the doctor continued.

"I think, at best, I can get you to where you have very minor pain once a week. For the most part, you're probably going to have to learn to live in chronic pain."

We thanked the doctor for his time and decided we would get a second opinion. We respectfully told him we wouldn't accept that diagnosis and instead would trust Jesus to heal her. He thought we were nuts. To be honest, we felt like we were a little bit crazy ourselves, but we want to live by faith, even when it contradicts all the facts! Nothing makes you question what you believe more than an appointment like that. We kept taking communion and decided we were going to fast.

At this point, we were about seven months into this, and it seemed like no end was in sight. I was fighting to keep my trust in Jesus and was extremely discouraged, to say the least. All the while, we felt stuck not knowing what to do. When it's you who are going through the trial, it's a lot easier to keep yourself encouraged. When it's someone you love and it seems as if there's nothing you can do, you feel helpless, and that's just how I felt. So we found another doctor. This one was a believer in Jesus and seemed hopeful that this was just an obstacle and that we would overcome it together. He sent us back to physical therapy to try again.

A couple weeks in, it had taken a turn for the worst. We were never really sure if Sarahbeth would be able to get up and walk from day to day without being in crazy pain. One day, while I was at work, she called me crying. She had tried to take a quick trip to the grocery store and the nerve shot pain down her leg in such an intense way she was sitting in the parking lot unable to get up. E was in the area, so she went and helped her up and back to the house where I would meet them. It was a breaking moment for me.

After I made sure beautiful Sarahbeth was comfortable and okay, I went for a walk around our neighborhood. This walk was so that I could tell Jesus how mad I was at Him for not healing my bride and that I didn't think He was very big after all. I was tired of taking communion and felt as if prayer was a hoax. I said some things on that walk to Jesus that probably aren't appropriate to write on these pages. I was letting Him know how I really felt, as if He didn't already know. I was pointing the finger at Him and giving Him all the blame. After I was done throwing my fit, I broke. I began to cry and begged Him for help, asking if He would please just heal my bride. Sometimes it takes getting alone in a secret place with Jesus to really get real with Him, and then, by nature, that's how you also build history with Him. Or maybe it's how He builds history with you. Either way, I had never been so honest with Him before. The same way I heard Him speak at that cold windy track meet; I heard Him on that summer day on Wilshire Blvd. It was the same loud voice that came like a whisper and rang throughout my whole heart.

"I am going to heal Sarahbeth. And I am going to do it my way!"

When Jesus speaks it will sober you up. You can also believe there is always a second voice that comes that tells you you're crazy and that Jesus doesn't speak. That's not His voice, but sometimes it sounds very convincing. So I opened up my Bible to John 10. Remember, John 10 is the chapter where Jesus is telling us about His voice and how His sheep know it. Sometimes I read John 10 when I need faith to believe what He said. It helps remind me to be a believer who believes and to lean on His words. However, when I read it this time, there was a section that jumped off the page and seemed to speak to me exactly where I was.

> *Then the Jews surrounded Him and said to Him, "How long do You keep us in doubt?* ***If You are the Christ, tell us plainly.****" Jesus answered them, "I told you, and you do not believe. The works that I do in My Father's name, they bear witness of Me. But you do not believe, because you are not of My sheep, as I said to you. My sheep hear My voice, and I know them, and they follow Me. And I give them eternal life, and they shall never perish; neither shall anyone snatch them out of My hand. My Father, who has given them to Me, is greater than all; and no one is able to snatch them out of My Father's hand. I and My Father are one." Then the Jews* ***took up stones again to stone Him****. Emphasis added.*
>
> John 10:24-31

Have you ever tried to stone Jesus? The Pharisees did. Here, Jesus is sharing words of life that will trickle through history forever, but they don't like what He is saying. Now remember, these are the same Pharisees that could not receive Jesus nor His words because they had big boxes constructed around what their image of the Messiah looked like. Let me show you how this passage came alive to me.

In verse 24, they come to Jesus and say to Him, *"Hey! How long will you keep us in this situation. Tell us. Are you the Christ or not?"* He says in verse 25 that He has already told them that He is and that they didn't believe. Isn't that crazy? At some point Jesus was sharing and said, "*Everybody, listen up, I am the Christ!*" Yet they didn't listen, and they didn't believe. So He is telling them that they aren't believers who believe, but to the ones who are, they will never be snatched from His hand. The Pharisees don't like this, and they get really mad. They didn't know what to do with their anger, so they picked up stones to stone Jesus.

How does this relate? Well, thanks for asking. The same way the Jews were asking Jesus how long they would be in that situation that "He had put them in" (quotations imply sarcasm because they were just really blaming Him for their own frustration), I was asking Jesus how long we would be in our situation with my beautiful bride's pain. Just like they wanted to be told plainly if He was the Christ, I wanted Him to tell me plainly if He was a healer.

Do you see it in verse 24? "*If you are _____, tell us plainly.*" Fill in the blank with what aspect of who the Bible tells us He is that we often struggle with. For me, it was Him as a healer.

When the outcome didn't play out like I thought, I started throwing stones. It wasn't physical stones like the Jews would throw, it was stones of frustration, blame, and unbelief in the form of harsh words. I threw the worst kind of stones; I threw stones in my heart. That day on that walk around the neighborhood, I too, just like the Pharisees, picked up stones to stone Him. I think a lot of Christians do this when we walk through trials where there is a seed of unbelief in our hearts and a certain circumstance finds that plot of ground to land on. The seed of unbelief grows into a massive weed of frustration and anger, and then, sooner or later, we point our finger at Jesus and give Him the blame. The beautiful thing is repentance is like a bulldozer that will rip that weed right up and a big Jesus loves to drive that bulldozer. I dropped the stones, and I picked up faith. His words that day became an anchor to attach every bit of disappointment and frustration to. I came home and shared with Sarahbeth about my conversation with Jesus, and together we thanked Him for the breakthrough that we hadn't yet received.

A couple weeks later I was scheduled to preach at our Sunday morning service. I preached a message titled "Faith Through Friction" and talked about throwing stones at Jesus. I shared about the trial we had been going through and how right in the middle of friction, Jesus was authoring faith. Of course, several people came up after service to pray over Sarahbeth. She didn't get healed that day, but we weren't discouraged. We knew what He had said: *I am going to heal Sarahbeth. And I am going to do it my way!* That next morning I received an email, and this is what it said.

> *Hello,*
> *My name is Briana & I just wanted to reach out to say how much this ministry encourages me, especially recently, in many different ways. I was diagnosed with Cerebral Palsy as a baby, so my whole life has been a difficult challenge physically; however, being 26 now, I've realized that even in the rough moments, my life is still a beautiful journey! Every day though, I continue to believe for complete healing in my body, especially when the pain is so intense & feels unbearable. In those moments, it's hard to keep going, but The Lord is so gracious & always helps me through. He did that this week through listening to the sermon from*

this Sunday at your church. I believe the speaker said his name was Aaron & everything that he spoke about is what I needed to hear & hold onto this week, as it's been an extremely difficult week for me physically. Thank you to this ministry for being obedient to The Holy Ghost & creating a space for Him to move!

God bless,
Briana

That same day I reached back out to Briana to hear her story. She had a similar experience to beautiful Sarahbeth except for her it had been twenty-six years long. Not seven months. She had been prayed for her entire life and had yet to be healed from cerebral palsy. I'm not going to put my lab coat and scrubs back on to explain cerebral palsy to you, but just know that for Briana it means she has to use a walker to get around. We talked on the phone about how Jesus isn't intimidated by her diagnosis, and we prayed together. Briana shared how she desired to be in ministry herself and would maybe one day come and visit Dallas. That one day came not many months after our phone call. Briana flew to Dallas and spent a week experiencing our community. Beautiful Sarahbeth and I took her lunch one afternoon and we got to hear all about how Jesus had been encouraging her since that day she listened to the sermon I preached. She again expressed that she wanted to be in ministry and that her dream was to go to Africa as a missionary. She had several challenges she would have to overcome to make a trip like that with her diagnosis, and several people she would have to convince to let her go. Instead of throwing stones at Jesus because she hadn't been healed, she was letting Him author faith. We prayed that it would happen in His timing and shortly after Briana traveled back home.

Every once in a while, I would get an email from her about how she was having a challenging day physically and could use prayer. She would always mention that sermon about having faith through friction - the one Jesus had given me that day I stopped throwing stones. Eventually, I got another email from Briana. It was one I wasn't expecting. In this one, she informed me that she would be moving to Africa very soon to be a missionary. Despite her condition, she was going to follow Jesus where He was authoring faith to go. We wrote Briana a letter of encouragement to open while she's in Africa and sent it to her. She's inspired our faith.

A couple of weeks after the "Faith Through Friction" sermon, Sarahbeth felt like the Lord asked her to go on a detox. For the next three months she would go without sugar, dairy, and rarely have meat. During that detox it seemed as if her sciatica symptoms disappeared just as quickly as they came. By the end of the three months, she was completely pain free and to this day, it hasn't returned. The crazy thing is, about a year after she had been healed, beautiful Sarahbeth had a dream that our church's kid's pastor had sciatica. That next morning, we went to church and saw her limping down the kid's hallway. Sarahbeth shared the dream with her and laid hands on her leg to pray for her. Right then and there, the sciatica pain left and never came back. What seemed as if it hadn't worked so many times for my bride, God did through her for someone else. That's just the thing about His way, it's not ours. Our way is often quick and painless. In fact, very few would choose His way. The Israelites way out of Egypt and into the promised land would've only taken eleven days. The Lord's way took forty years. We often think *the way* is a means to get to a destination, but I think *the way* is actually a lot more about being with Jesus and learning about who He is on the journey. Isaiah 55:8-9 explains this a little better. It says:

> "For My thoughts are not your thoughts,
> **Nor are your ways My ways,**" says the Lord.
> "For as the heavens are higher than the earth,
> So are **My ways higher than your ways,**
> And My thoughts than your thoughts." Emphasis added.

If He hadn't led them out of the wilderness His way, the children of Israel would've never seen Him provide water out of a rock. They wouldn't have seen Him bring manna from Heaven. They wouldn't have received the Ten Commandments. The Lord's way taught them that He is their provider in all things. His way is always higher and grander than our way. His way is about weaving things together so that we learn something about who He is, and in the process, we see just how big His heart is. I think that's what Paul is talking about in Romans 8:28.

> And we know that all things work together for good to
> those who love God, to those who are the called according
> to His purpose.

Here is what I know. I know that despite our conditions, circumstances, or diagnoses, Jesus is bigger than them all. No situation in the Bible intimidated Jesus, and I don't think ours does either. But here is what I don't know. I don't know why Sarahbeth had sciatica or why Briana was born with cerebral palsy. I don't know why our kid's pastor was healed in a moment and Sarahbeth had to do a three-month detox. Maybe if I tried hard enough, I could create a structure of human reasoning—like a box—big enough to put around Jesus and explain why some people get healed and others don't. To be honest, I think that's just a passive aggressive way of throwing stones. Quite frankly, I don't think it's even about what we know or don't know. I think it's about walking with Jesus His way, learning something new about who He is, and watching as He weaves together a story that's a lot bigger than *our way* would allow. Our way wouldn't have allowed for Briana to be encouraged or sent to Africa. In fact, our way wouldn't have involved Briana at all. His way is about making all things work together for good and connecting us to something that's a lot bigger than we are. That doesn't mean we stop praying for healing or start believing that God would rather we be in pain so that He can teach us a lesson. I don't think He teaches that way. Storms are just a normal part of the forecast. It means in the middle of friction, there is an invitation to stop throwing stones at Jesus and let Him author faith to go His way. Besides, *He is the way*. Going that direction, you get Him, and if you get Him, you better believe something amazing is soon to happen.

Sometimes when we think of Briana, we stop and ask Jesus to be bigger than He has ever been to her before and heal her body. Sometimes we talk about maybe the whole reason we went through this was just so Jesus could use Sarahbeth's story to encourage Briana and get her to Africa. I think sometimes we put healing in a box and say it has to come in a specific way or it's not Him. I don't think the blind man in John 9 would've given a lesson on healing saying the way is to spit in dirt and then put it in his eye. No, that was Jesus' way. I also bet that the blind man was about ready to throw stones before He realized it worked. Here is the point, at the end of the day, stones aren't supposed to be in our hands, we're supposed to be in His. And if you're in His hands, then no one can snatch you out. Not sciatica and not cerebral palsy. I don't think stones can snatch you out either. You never see a moment when Jesus was scared of those who wanted to stone Him. If you let Him, He will just use it as an opportunity to teach you something about His heart. Nonetheless, it is in the place of His hands that all things are worked together. That's just His way and it's the way He wants to lead us. It's the better way, anyways. He gets to be a lot bigger when we go down His path. The cool thing is, He is big enough to lead you His way regardless of what life throws at you. He isn't intimidated by your circumstance, and He won't turn you away if you get real with Him. I bet He is even moving right now in your life in ways you don't know, and to see it, all you have to do is stop throwing stones.

"Jesus, thank you that YOU are the way! I repent for the times I have thrown stones in my heart at you when things did not turn out like I thought or hoped. Will you break any box of unbelief I have in my heart and give me the faith to know your way is higher than mine? I trust you and believe that you are who you say you are!"

Chapter 9

LET'S PUT THAT BONE BACK TOGETHER

"...and He healed them all!"

Let's talk about healing. One of the biggest things Jesus was known for while He was on the earth were the miracles that He would perform on the sick and the injured and even the dead. In fact, it was what drew the crowds. Don't get me wrong. I think Jesus' sermons were fire. If it were modern day, His podcast would be viral and preachers across the planet would be attempting to mimic His methods. Regardless of how He preached, that's not what brought the multitude. It was His signs and wonders performed on the sick. Many would travel far and wide to meet this miracle worker and many would do bizarre things just to get in front of Him for a chance to be healed. There was one lady who pushed her way through anyone and everyone just to touch Jesus' clothes in an attempt to be healed. One group of friends even took a jackhammer to someone else's roof and created a DIY elevator to lower their friend in front of Jesus. All of this because, even if they couldn't tell you anything else about Him, they could tell you one thing: Jesus of Nazareth is a healer.

In chapter 15 of Matthew's account of the gospels, he writes this in verse 30 and 31:

> *Then great multitudes came to Him, having with them the lame, blind, mute, maimed, and many others; and they laid them down at Jesus' feet, **and He healed them**. So, the multitude marveled when they saw the mute speaking, the maimed made whole, the lame walking, and the blind seeing; and they glorified the God of Israel. Emphasis added.*

The great multitudes were coming to Him, and they were bringing their sick and lame. There was a miracle worker they had heard of, and if it was true, they had to see for themselves. Healing is what caused His name to spread and His fame to grow. By the way, according to the NLT version, He healed them all, not just some or the ones who got there first. However, at the end of Luke 5:15, this specific translation uses the word *all*, because any and all who came around this man named Jesus found their broken bodies put back together. It wasn't just something only one of the gospels portrays but it was a central theme in all four of them. In case Matthew wasn't very convincing above, let's look at how Luke said it in chapter 5:12-15.

> *And it happened when He was in a certain city, that behold, a man who was full of leprosy saw Jesus; and he fell on his face and implored Him, saying, "Lord, if You are willing, you can make me clean." Then He put out His hand and touched him, saying, "I am willing; be cleansed." Immediately the leprosy left him. And He charged him to tell no one, "But go and show yourself to the priest, and make an*

*offering for your cleansing, as a testimony to them, just as Moses commanded." However, **the report went around concerning Him all the more; and great multitudes came** together to hear, **and to be healed by Him** of their infirmities. Emphasis added.*

A report went out: *"There is one among us who is a healer."* And as the report spread, the crowd grew. It's safe to say if there was one thing Jesus was known for in His time, it was healing. If it was the case then, it should be the case today. If it was a priority to Jesus then, I am not sure why it wouldn't be a priority to Him now. I think many of our approaches to Jesus are like this man from Luke 5 that comes to Jesus and says *"Lord, if you're willing."* But believers who believe know His response: *"I am willing."* There is no one in the Gospels that we see Jesus turn away, and there is no one that was prayed for that didn't receive breakthrough. Although, in Mark 8 there was one blind man who Jesus had to pray for twice. He got his sight the first time Jesus prayed, but the new prescription for his eyes were just a little off, so Jesus had to pray a second time so he wouldn't mistake men for trees. However, He was still healed. There are twenty-two recorded healings in the Gospels, and all of them were unique. For the centurion's daughter, she had been sick just a few days. For the lady who couldn't stop bleeding, it had been a twelve-year battle. The crippled man at the pool of Bethesda had lain there for thirty-eight years. The boy whose seizures would throw him into the water and the fire was born that way. I could go on, but the point is, they were all healed, and because of this,

Jesus' fame was spreading, and it was bringing the masses. It was even healing that got Jesus killed. In John 11, Jesus would raise Lazarus from the dead. It was one of the most profound healings Jesus would perform. Lazarus' sickness had gotten so bad that it took his life. We know the story; Jesus would come days after the grave-side ceremony had ended and heal the man who was un-healable. For how could sickness be healed in a dead man? However, Jesus was about to show them just how big He was, for He is big indeed, and He is always willing. Sure enough, after just one prayer from the mouth of our healer, the dead man received life again and walked out of the tomb that had been his new home for the past four days. After he had risen, Lazarus went home to shower off the smell of death he had been sitting in, and the report of all that had just taken place began to spread. This is the account of Jesus healing Lazarus in John 11:46-48 and 53-54:

> *But some of them went away to the Pharisees and told them the things Jesus did. Then the chief priests and the Pharisees gathered a council and said, "What shall we do? For this Man works many signs. If we let Him alone like this, everyone will believe in Him, and the Romans will come and take away both our place and nation…."*
>
> ***Then, from that day on, they plotted to put Him to death***. *Therefore, Jesus no longer walked openly among the Jews, but went from there into the country near the wilderness, to a city called Ephraim, and there remained with His disciples. Emphasis added.*

This time, Jesus had gone too far and revealed Himself to be too big. This is the plot that would lead Jesus to the cross and take His life. To be honest, I am not sure the Pharisees put a whole lot of thought into this. I mean, if the guy is raising others from the dead, then obviously death is no rival to Him. However, the Pharisees didn't fully think it through and again, we know the story. Just like He raised Lazarus from the dead, He would rise too. I know He had to die to *"fulfill all scripture"* and all of that, but we aren't talking about deep theological things here, were talking about Jesus' reputation. He is known for being the healer, for the healer He is.

At the end of the spring semester, the school of ministry in our church ends the year by dividing into teams and going on mission trips across the nation. Beautiful Sarahbeth and I got to lead one of the trips as the school wrapped up its debut year. We would lead a team of sixteen to Phoenix, Arizona. Over the next ten days, we would spend almost every waking hour together as a team, ministering at different services and churches as well as the city at large. We all bunked up in a two-story Airbnb and pretty quickly we got really close. One of the things we made mandatory as a team is that we would start and end every day together praying over one another. We knew there would be lots of opportunities to get upset with one another or even just grow weary from doing good because of how packed full our schedule was. So, if we were going to pray as a team in public, we knew to stay open hearted and keep our eyes on a big Jesus, we needed to pray together in private. At the end of the day, we would always ask this same question: *Who needs prayer tonight?* It was so refreshing seeing our team let down their walls with one another and invite Jesus into our team meetings. Side note: even ministers need to be ministered to at times. One of the nights we were praying together, most of us were in tears. The only way to describe the environment was as if Jesus Himself had walked right into the room. It was, in fact, that He had. It felt just like that day on that windy track field, except this time I wasn't experiencing it alone. I was with a room full of people who felt it too. We stopped asking who needed prayer and just started praying over one another. It just seemed right in that environment. We would choose someone in the room, and all come around them to encourage and pray over them. Once prayer ended for one person, we would move onto pray for another. Many of us felt as if the Lord was speaking to secret prayer requests and bringing life to that one area that only He could minister to. We all knew Jesus was in the room. Eventually, He made it to Kate.

Kate is full of life and brings a lot of joy to whatever room she is in. She loves people and lives her life like she believes Jesus is really big. She's always one of the first to jump in and serve however she can, while carrying a smile the entire time she does it. I asked beautiful Sarahbeth to describe her in one word. She chose the word *vivacious*, which means attractively lively and animated. Anyone who's ever been around Kate would know this to be true. Before traveling to Phoenix together, we only knew Kate by one thing. She wore one of those big black medical boots on her right foot. A few months earlier she had been with her friends at home. They had music playing in the living room and Kate decided she would teach them a dance move from her high school drill team. The tutorial didn't go according to plan, and by accident, Kate's foot high-fived the edge of her couch. (Maybe now you know what we mean by vivacious.) When her foot met the couch, she broke her 5th metatarsal straight in half. Ouch! The Doctor prescribed her the boot and she was to be in it for eight weeks. That eight weeks turned into three and a half months. Because of the uniqueness of the break, the boot wasn't helping, and Kate had been living in level eight pain daily. After the designated time in the boot, the doctor looked it over and suggested extending the time she would wear it until after she returned from our trip in Phoenix. The doctor was recommending surgery.

When it came time to pray for Kate that night in our Airbnb, one of our team members jumped right in and took the lead.

"I just can't shake this, I keep imagining Jesus kneeling down in front of you saying 'Hey, Kate! Let's put that bone back together!' I feel like were supposed to pray for your foot." She said with full confidence as she continued. "I also keep thinking about that old kid's song. 'The hip bone's connected to the shoulder bone,' remember that one? Let's all sing it over her foot as a prayer!"

Okay, so if you're like me, this is one of those moments when you pull out the phrase: *That's weird! Could be God. It probably is.* So, we Googled the lyrics and all got around Kate to pray over her foot.

> ♪ *"Your hip bone's connected from your thigh bone*
> *Your thigh bone's connected from your knee bone*
> *Your knee bone's connected from your leg bone*
> *Your leg bone's connected from your ankle bone*
> *Your ankle bone's connected from your heel bone*
> *Your heel bone's connected from your foot bone*
> *I hear the word of the Lord"* ♪

Now, let me tell you, we all felt like we had lost our minds. Nonetheless, I think that was the point, because faith will make you feel that way sometimes. Let me also remind you that the room felt like it was smothered in the presence of Jesus. If you've never experienced that, it feels as if Heaven is in the room and nothing else seems to matter other than Jesus. We all looked at Kate as tears ran down her face. The next thing we know, she was taking off her boot. This is how she recounted that day in her own words.

> *While my foot was being prayed for, I felt joyful. It was like I all of a sudden, I expected my foot to be healed. I was ready to fight for my healing no matter how long it took. Once Sarahbeth started singing the bone song over my foot, I felt heat start from the top of my head to the foot that was broken. I felt heat where the broken bone was.*

So Kate felt heat in her foot and she removed the boot to attempt to walk on it. As she did, she informed us that she had zero pain but a lot of soreness. That evening, we all went to bed full of faith for Kate's foot. The next day, we got up to leave, and as we all piled into our cars, we noticed Kate had on both shoes and no boot. She was pain free. We were running a little behind that day, so most of us forgot to acknowledge her foot and see how it was doing. Trips with big groups like that one have the ability to keep you busy and going from place to place. Before you know it, you are at the end of your trip and you still need to find time to recap all the testimonies that have taken place. That was the case with this one, and before you knew it, we were on the way to the airport, and we had still yet to process with

Kate how her foot was doing. It had been about a week since that night we sang the bone song, and we had hardly noticed she had left her boot behind. However, as we walked through the airport terminal, one of the students on our team grabbed our attention and put our focus on Kate. She was about fifteen yards in front of us, merrily skipping through the terminal while she carried her black medical boot in her left hand. It had been over a week since she wore it or even felt pain. Jesus had healed her. What she came into Phoenix wearing on her right foot, she left carrying it in her hand. She stashed it into the overhead compartment on the plane and stretched out her pain free foot. That bone had been put back together. The presence of Jesus was truly present that night and when Jesus comes around, He is sure to heal the sick, the injured, and the hurting. It's what He is known for.

Not one person in the Gospels that came to Jesus in need of healing left without it. He healed them all. Not only that, but when He ascended back to Heaven, He gave us a pretty clear command. He says in Mark 16:14-18:

> Later He appeared to the eleven as they sat at the table; and He rebuked their unbelief and hardness of heart, because they did not believe those who had seen Him after He had risen. And He said to them, "Go into all the world and preach the gospel to every creature. He who believes and is baptized will be saved; but he who does not believe will be condemned. And these signs will follow those who believe: In My name they will cast out demons; they will speak with new tongues; they will take up serpents; and if

they drink anything deadly, it will by no means hurt them;
they will lay hands on the sick, and they will recover."
Emphasis added.

I have heard a lot of people take this passage and shrink how big Jesus is by saying that this was for the apostles only. The thing is, I read here where Jesus says to lay hands on the sick so that they are healed in His name, but I have yet to read where Jesus says to stop praying that the sick will be healed in His name. I think those people have maybe just forgotten that healing and signs and wonders is kind of what He is known for. Maybe they have an experience where they haven't stopped throwing stones or maybe they just have never known His reputation as a healer. Regardless, one of Jesus's last commands while He walked the earth in the flesh was to lay hands on the sick. Something I have learned is that it isn't us who are healers, it's Him. We just get to believe what He said. When someone gets healed by your prayer, Jesus get all the credit. I have also learned sometimes that His way is not our way, and if someone doesn't get healed, He gets none of the blame. We simply just keep being believers who believe, and we lay hands and pray again. What we aren't supposed to do, is stop relating Jesus to healing. That would be silly; He has a reputation for it. Think about it this way, wouldn't it be a little strange if we stopped relating Tom Brady with football or Michael Jordan with basketball? Of course it would, it's what they're known for! What they are known for is why they draw crowds to stadiums and arenas. Likewise, it's how Jesus draws the crowds to Himself. Even in the Old Testament writings, when Jesus as the Messiah was prophesied, healing was mentioned. It has always been a theme that was connected to who the Messiah would be. Take a look at Isaiah 53:4-6.

Surely He has borne our griefs
And carried our sorrows;
Yet we esteemed Him stricken,
Smitten by God, and afflicted.
*But He was **wounded for our transgressions**,*
*He was **bruised for our iniquities**;*
The chastisement for our peace was upon Him,
*And **by His stripes we are healed**.*
All we like sheep have gone astray;
We have turned, every one, to his own way;
And the Lord has laid on Him the iniquity of us all. Emphasis added.

Who is *He* that this passage is referring to? It's Jesus. You can go back to that paragraph of scripture and replace the word *He* with *Jesus* and re-read the text and you get a profound revelation of who Jesus was always prophesied to be. At the cross, He fulfilled this very passage. Jesus was wounded, beaten, whipped, pierced, and gruesomely tortured for your sins and ultimately for your healing. The body of Jesus was broken so that yours and mine and every other one that we lay hands on would be whole! Jesus paid a high price with His own blood so that healing would be available to all mankind. Have you ever realized that, before Jesus ever preached a message, He healed people. Before Jesus went to the cross, He healed people. Even after Jesus ascended to be with the Father, the next part of the story in the book of Acts is full of His leaders healing people in Jesus' name. It's who He is and what He is like; He heals the sick and restores the injured.

You see, healing is not a sermon to preach or a theology to argue; healing is a part of our Messiah's nature! A big Jesus doesn't talk about healing as if it is a thing of the past or something that ended with the leadership of the early church. Oh no! When a big Jesus walks in the room and there is a person with their 5th metatarsal broken straight in half, He gets down in front of them and says *"Let's put that bone back together!"*

"Jesus, thank you that YOU are the ultimate healer! I believe your body was broken so that ours could be whole! Would you break any boxes I have around you as a healer? Lord, help my unbelief and open my eyes to see that you are both willing and able to heal! Give me the faith to lay hands on the sick and watch you show up in power and love!"

Chapter 10

IT ALL HAPPENED AT WALMART

Jesus' favorite place to perform miracles is outside the temple!

L et's stay in Phoenix a little longer. I would be doing you an absolute disservice bringing up that trip if I didn't tell you about
Walmart. I don't know about you, but Walmart isn't my store
of choice. I am more of Kroger or Whole Foods type of guy for
groceries, and if I am looking for household goods, then Target
is the place for me. Walmart is usually a last resort. Don't get me
wrong, I love their prices. It's just seems like every time I go, the
checkout lines are the Lord's tool to produce within me greater
levels of patience, and you're sure to run into an experience that
you probably think belongs on YouTube. Target always seems to
be in and out, hassle free, and you certainly cannot beat the produce at Whole Foods. However, you also cannot beat the prices at
Walmart, so make your pick. I don't think Jesus had a preference
of where He went to shop. I think He would go to the places
where people needed the most breakthrough. I don't think He
was concerned with hassle free or worried about having to wait
in checkout lines. In fact, I think most of the time He went to

the places that His disciples thought were far from hassle free. Actually, if you read the Gospels, you'll see that every one of Jesus' miracles were done outside of the temple, not in it. Don't get me wrong, Jesus was often in the temple. Normally, He was flipping tables or rebuking the leaders that led it, but He was in the temple a lot. Sometimes He would teach to the multitudes and others He would read the scriptures. Nonetheless, when you read about the miracles He performed, you'll see that the scene of the crime was outside the four walls of the church. Usually they were in places like Walmart, places that didn't seem to be hassle free. I bet if Jesus walked through Walmart today, He would cause a lot of moments that should belong on YouTube or TikTok. He probably wouldn't mind waiting in the checkout line either. I bet by the time it was His turn to pay, He would be able to tell you everyone's name that He stood in line with and all about their lives.

On one of the last days of our trip to Phoenix, we were going over our group finances and we realized that we had significantly stayed under budget. We were so far from being in the red that we were blue. It's a really good feeling when you're leading a trip with a large team and there isn't a burden of finances. However, we were at the tail end of our trip, so we put our heads together to come up with a creative way to make sure the money went to good use. Our Airbnb was down the street from a large super Walmart, the one on east Chaparral road. We thought it would be cool to go and pay for people's groceries and tell them about how big Jesus is in the process. If Walmart was an interesting place to be, why not add to the excitement. We all loved the idea and decided to do it treasure hunt style.

Now, in case you've never heard of a treasure hunt, I'll explain. A treasure hunt is an easy way to practice faith and tell people about Jesus. Let me give you scripture. In Acts 9, Saul of Tarsus, the one we all know as the Paul, who wrote much of the New Testament, is at the height of his conquest of killing Christians. However, he has just had an encounter with the presence of Jesus on the road to Damascus, where Jesus asks him, *"Why are you persecuting me?"* A great light flashes from Heaven and blinds Saul, and Jesus instructs him to go into the city and wait until he is told what to do. So he is led by his servants into the city, and for the next three days, Saul just waits on Jesus. We'll pick up the story in verse 10-12 and 15-18.

> *Now there was a certain disciple at Damascus named Ananias; and to him the Lord said in a vision, "Ananias." And he said, "Here I am, Lord." So the Lord said to him, "Arise and **go to the street called Straight**, and inquire at the house of Judas **for one called Saul of Tarsus**, for behold, he is praying. And in a vision he has seen a man named Ananias coming in and putting his hand on him, **so that he might receive his sight.**"*

> *...But the Lord said to him, "Go, for he is a chosen vessel of Mine to bear My name before Gentiles, kings, and the children of Israel. For I will show him how many things he must suffer for My name's sake." And Ananias went his way and entered the house; and laying his hands on him he said, "Brother Saul, the Lord Jesus, who appeared to you on the road as you came, has sent me that you may receive your sight*

and be filled with the Holy Spirit." Immediately there fell
from his eyes something like scales, and he received his sight at
once; and he arose and was baptized. Emphasis added.

Meet Ananias! The man who goes on the first treasure hunt. Fun fact: this is the only time in scripture that he is mentioned. Here in Acts 9, you see the Lord tell him three things in verse 11. One, where to go. Jesus tells Ananias to go to a *street called Straight*. Two, who to pray for. He is instructed to find and pray for *a man called Saul of Tarsus*. And three, Jesus tells Ananias what issue to pray for, *so that he might receive his sight*. He follows the direction of Jesus and goes to find his treasure, or should I say, Jesus' treasure. If it weren't for Ananias, Saul might never have become Paul. If it weren't for Ananias, Paul wouldn't have written two-thirds of the New Testament. If it weren't for Ananias, who knows if Saul would have received his sight back and taken the gospel to the gentiles.

This is how you model a treasure hunt. You take time in prayer and ask Jesus where to go, who to pray for, and what to pray for. Just like in Acts 9. It takes faith to believe that Jesus will lead you to find your treasure and this exercise is a great way to practice it. So as a team, we broke up into four separate groups and I set a five-minute timer on my phone. During those five minutes, we take time individually to pray and ask Jesus to show us our treasure. I always tell those I do treasure hunts with to get out a pen and paper or to take notes on their phone and write down anything and everything that comes across their imagination. For instance, if in that five minutes of prayer your mind thinks of a red T-shirt, then write it down. If your imagination puts the name Joel on the forefront of your mind, then write it down. If, while you're praying, you can't stop thinking of that coffee shop down the road, then you write it down. So on and so forth. At the end of the five minutes, you get together with your group and compare notes. Almost always there is a correlation or a theme. You could say it makes a treasure map. The next part is the fun part. You practice faith and go find your treasure. It's pretty cool when you go to that coffee shop down the road and there's a man wearing a red T-shirt. It's even cooler when his name happens to be Joel and you get to show him your notes and tell him how Jesus led you to him. Then, if he lets you pray for him, maybe he'll give his life to Jesus, or his family will have breakthrough. Maybe *something like scales* will fall off his eyes and for the first time ever he'll see a big Jesus. Hopefully now you understand the concept of a treasure hunt. So let's get back to Phoenix.

During our five-minute timer we all prayed that Jesus would lead us to His treasure. We all had something out to take notes with, and before you knew it, the timer was going off. We separated into our groups and started sharing. In my group, including myself, there were four of us. We circled up and started sharing what we wrote down. One of our teammates said she wrote down: **Spanish speaking**. Another girl in our group had written down: **running shoes**. And another said: **Maryland**. For me, I had written down: **basket full of items**. So, our treasure map was to go to the Walmart down the road and find the person who was Spanish speaking and from Maryland. We figured they would have a basket full of items, and maybe at the top would be a pair of running shoes. We hopped in the car and drove to Walmart. If we found our treasure, we were going to tell them all about Jesus and offer to pay for whatever was in their cart.

You always feel a little crazy walking around a public place looking at strangers as if you are the FBI and they are your suspect. You feel even more crazy if you ask that guy in the red T-shirt if his name is Joel and he tells you no. Nonetheless, you're practicing faith. I'm sure Ananias felt crazy walking into the room to pray in Jesus' name for the man who killed people that believed in Jesus. If he got it wrong, he would be killed. If we got it wrong, we would only look silly. So we walked into Walmart acting like we had a lot more confidence then we probably did. At the front the store, we saw a lady with a cart that looked like she spoke Spanish. The problem was her cart was empty. So we passed her by without saying a word and kept looking. We decided to go to the shoe section, thinking maybe *running shoes* was a hint to the location we would find the one from *Maryland*. When we got there, however, the aisle was empty! So again, we kept searching. We made our way around Walmart and into the toy section. As we passed the baby aisle, we noticed the same lady that we had seen at the front of the store with her empty cart. As we walked by, we overheard her speaking to her toddler son. She was speaking Spanish.

"Let's ask her what her name is and see if she is the treasure!" We began to whisper to one another. We all agreed, and we approached her.

"Hola, ma'am. Cómo estás?" That's Spanish for "how are you?" She could probably tell by my incredible American accent that my Spanish was bad enough to not be considered Spanish at all, because she answered back in English.

"I am good, thanks." She said, implying the fact that we were strangers, and she wasn't looking to get into conversation.

"This may seem strange, but we're looking for someone special. We love Jesus and we felt like He led us to Walmart tonight to find someone He wanted to bless. We felt like that person is you and we were wondering if we could pay for your entire cart." I said, fully committing and jumping all the way in. She only fit one out of four of our description of the treasure, but sometimes it's just about loving the one in front of you. However, Jesus was just getting ready to remind us how big He really is.

"Oh wow. I don't know!" she responded. "I am just looking for a toy for a family that I wanted to bless." She went on to tell us that the reason she was in the baby section was that she knew of a family that was living in poverty. The parents had four daughters and were living in a one-room studio. The youngest daughter was a newborn, and the family didn't have money to buy any essentials for the baby. This lady, who later told us her name was Anna, was wanting to buy a toy to take to the studio to give to the family. However, she informed us that money was a little bit tight for her own family, and she wasn't sure she could afford much. The more she told us about this family, the more her heart opened up.

"I really just wish I could do more." She mentioned to us. Our team all put our heads together and we had a thought. What if Jesus sent us to her to fill up her cart with essentials for this family?

What the heck! We're practicing faith, I thought as I gave the green light to our team to fill the cart up.

"Anna, I think were supposed to fill this cart up and pay for it for you. You tell us what the family needs, and if it fits in this cart, we'll buy it!"

She looked at us with wide eyes like she was in a dream and started to cry. She told us that she had prayed right before she entered Walmart that Jesus would help her find a way to bless this family. He was doing just that. Of course, she kept asking if we were sure and it was with big smiles that we kept reminding her we were! We walked around the store getting all kinds of stuff. We got clothes for each child and cooking pans for their kitchen. We got diapers and wet wipes, and we even got several toys. One basket quickly turned into two and before we knew it, we had them both filled all the way. The entire time, Anna was in tears, and the more we got to talking to her, the more she opened up.

"Where are you from?" We asked her. The conversation had begun to pick up and felt easy, but her answer stopped us right in our tracks.

"My family is from Maryland but we are living here in Phoenix now," She informed us. She had now hit three out of four of the treasure descriptions. She told us all about her family and how they had made it to Phoenix. Her parents had moved to the states from Colombia, and her brother wanted to be a pastor. As Anna told us about her family, she began to ask us to pray for her brother. Although he desired to be a pastor, he was in the middle of a two-year battle with anxiety and depression. It was currently so bad that he hadn't even gotten out of bed the past two weeks to eat. We told her that after we checked out, we would help her get everything to the car and then pray in the parking lot. Just as we finished getting everything we needed for the family from the studio, a man walked up to join us. His name was Pablo. Anna introduced us to her husband, and she explained the reason we were there and why we had two whole shopping carts full of stuff. He let out the most holy laugh as he gave us hugs. He said he couldn't believe what he was hearing.

"There is one more thing!" I said, right before we started making our way to check out.

"I know we filled up this cart for another family, but we want to bless you. So before we checkout, if there is anything in this store you want or need? We also want to get that!" I continued. At first, they said they were okay and that they didn't need anything. Nonetheless, they looked at each other like there was one thing and we could tell they were about to take us up on the offer.

"There is something." Anna said. "Our kids could really use new running shoes!"

That was it. Four out of four. Anna and Pablo were the treasure. At this point, I am not sure who was more blessed, them or us. We knew Jesus had led us to this Walmart because He wanted this couple to know how big He is. We walked over to the shoe section and let each of the kids pick out a couple pairs that they liked. We added them to the cart and headed to the register. At the checkout, we secretly grabbed a gift card and loaded it with a hundred dollars. After we got everything into their car, we told them we had one last gift. We gave them the gift card and told them it was specifically for the two of them to go out on a date night. Again, here came the tears.

"We haven't been out on a nice date to dinner in over two years." Pablo said to Anna as he looked at her with passionate eyes. We told them all about Jesus and then asked what all we could pray for. The big request was Anna's brother. So we gathered together and thanked Jesus for how we had met and asked Him to move in their family. We invited them to the service we would be leading the next day, and we hugged them goodbye. Just before we left, Anna told us that before tonight, she thought Jesus had given up on them. Now she knew He hadn't.

Now, we were all in awe of what Jesus had just done, but He still wasn't done with this family. The next day, as we were getting ready to start our service, we noticed a sweet elderly Spanish man who was walking around asking if he could talk to our team. We approached the man and introduced ourselves. He was Anna's father.

"Hi, you don't know me, but I am William. Anna is my daughter who you met last night at Walmart. I had to come meet you guys. I did the math, and right about the exact time you guys were praying in the parking lot, my son got up out of bed and, for the first time in two weeks, he had a smile on his face and he ate food." This may seem like a small thing, but what we didn't know is that every day for the past ten days, William had been asking Jesus to help his son. Jesus had done just that. We were all a mess as we watched William worship Jesus that day at the front of the room.

When Jesus would go out in public places, wild things would happen. It's still the same today. I love all of the things that happen in the church. There's salvation and teaching of the Word! We get to worship Jesus together with family and friends. The church is one of the most beautiful places to me because it is His house. Even so, a big Jesus likes to send people to places *like a street called Straight* because He loves to move outside the temple. We get to be His hands and feet and go pray for those that are His treasure. And a lot of the time, His treasures just haven't made it into the church yet. That's why He likes to go to them. Jesus says it like this in Matthew 15:12-14:

> *"What do you think? If a man has a hundred sheep, and one of them goes astray,* **does he not leave the ninety-nine and go to the mountains to seek the one that is straying***? And if he should find it, assuredly, I say to you, he rejoices more over that sheep than over the ninety-nine that did not go astray. Even so it is not the will of your Father who is in heaven that one of these little ones should perish. Emphasis added.*

It doesn't bother Jesus to go out of His way for the one. In fact, it brings Him great joy. That's why He says *when He finds it, He rejoices greatly*. The ninety-nine are normally all in the temple. So Jesus puts His hiking boots on and heads out to find the one. The exciting thing is, He uses us to do it, just like Ananias.

It always takes faith to pray for someone in public, and you might even end up looking silly. It might not be culturally accepted or politically correct, but that makes no difference to

Jesus, He doesn't mind if He is politically correct or in line with culture. He loves to move outside the temple. Sometimes you'll pray for healing, like for someone's sight to come back, or maybe you'll pray for a family that's living in poverty. Perhaps you'll pray for someone's brother who is in the middle of a two-year battle with anxiety and depression. Nonetheless, believers who believe know that when Jesus goes out in public, wild things happen. Like the kind of stuff that probably belongs on YouTube. I think it's because Jesus is too big to stay in the temple anyways. I'm sure if we ask Him, we will see Him touch people in Kroger or Whole Foods too. Maybe someone will give their life to Jesus in the middle of Target. It could be that maybe you even find yourself going to that coffee shop down the street to pray for that guy in the red T-shirt. His name doesn't even have to be Joel! It's all about practicing faith and letting Jesus be really big. I mean, come on. Anna and Pablo were in tears seeing how big Jesus is. He answered Anna's prayer before she could even leave the store and her brother received the breakthrough that their dad had been praying for. Not only that, but another family we didn't even get the chance to meet had two entire shopping carts full of items delivered straight to their doorstep. Jesus was showing Himself as really big to not only our team, but to two other families as well, because He loves to move in public places. I don't know if you have ever been like Ananias and went where Jesus told you to go or if you have ever prayed for people in public. I'm not sure if you've seen Jesus move outside the temple, but let me tell you, I have seen it firsthand, and it all happened at Walmart.

"Jesus, thank you that you are not confined to the four walls of the church! I believe that YOU love to minister to people through me. Would you break any boxes I have around how you show up and would you give me the faith to live boldly, expressing your power in public places!?"

Chapter 11

NEIGHBORHOOD LOVE

The love of Jesus is for your next-door neighbor!

One of the temptations that comes with working in full-time ministry is that, if you aren't careful, you can start to clock in and out of love. I don't mean you stop being a Christian once you leave the church and become a humbug to the world, but what I mean is that you can check out from people and stay to yourself. It's easy to turn off your love in the name of boundaries and forget that love is something that's never supposed to turn off. Don't get me wrong, boundaries are great, and without them you'll invite all sorts of frustrations into your home. Nonetheless, in Mark 12, the religious leaders of the day come to Jesus to try to catch Him in His words and expose Him as a fraud. Obviously, they just made fools of themselves and couldn't do it. However, they make one last attempt and Jesus responds by dropping one of the most profound truths in all of scripture.

Then one of the scribes came, and having heard them reasoning together, perceiving that He had answered them well, asked Him, "Which is the first commandment of all?" Jesus answered him, "The first of all the commandments is: 'Hear, O Israel, the Lord our God, the Lord is one. And you shall love the Lord your God with all your heart, with all your soul, with all your mind, and with all your strength.' This is the first commandment. And the second, like it, is this: **'You shall love your neighbor as yourself.' There is no other commandment greater than these."** *Emphasis added*

Mark 12:28-31

The question is this: *What is the greatest commandment?* Jesus responds by giving them a two-part answer. Love God with all your heart and love your neighbor as yourself. The first one is easy. God isn't hard to love. That is, unless you're throwing stones; but God is perfect. He is kind and compassionate. He is patient with us and leads us with His hand. He never leaves us, and in all things, you'll find that He is for you. He doesn't say mean words or yell at you when you get it wrong. He doesn't get His feelings hurt when we mess up or do something incorrect. In fact, He is the best encourager I know. Someone like that is easy to love. You don't have to worry about rejection or Him not loving you back. He is always leaning into our lives and never annoyed. However, loving our neighbor is sometimes a challenge. I remember one time I had a neighbor put a sign in my front yard of the presidential candidate that I didn't plan on voting for. Another time, a different neighbor accidentally shot out the back window of my truck with a BB gun. Neighbors can be difficult to love. Even so, as difficult as it may be, the second half of the greatest commandment is to love our neighbors as ourselves.

What it doesn't say is to "love your neighbor when it's convenient for you" or to "love your neighbor if their beliefs are the same." No, that's not what Jesus says. That means, when I answer the front door to my neighbor informing me that the window to my truck is shattered, I am supposed to love. It also means when I come home to find a political sign in my yard, I am not supposed to go make a scene. I am supposed to love my neighbor. It's the greatest commandment. I don't turn off my love or withhold it from my neighbors because I had a long day at the office. In fact, it's quite the opposite. Loving our neighbor is top priority. Sure, *neighbor* is poetry for whoever is in front of you. The cashier at the grocery store is your neighbor. So is your waiter or the driver in front of you that is on his phone and hasn't realized the traffic light turned green. Your co-worker and boss are *your neighbor*. I am pretty sure all of mankind falls into the category of neighbor, but I also like to take scripture literally and make it as simple as I can. That means Jesus is referring to the young college students that live in the house next door that throw parties on weeknights. My actual neighbors. They aren't supposed to get the sloppy seconds of love because I gave the first of it away in a pastoral meeting. Love doesn't work like that. It's not a switch that you turn on and off based on how your day went. Love for one another is what is supposed to set us apart from the world. That's what Jesus says in John 13:34-35.

> *A new commandment I give to you, that you love one an-other; as I have loved you, that you also love one another.* **By this all will know that you are My disciples, if you have love for one another.** *Emphasis added.*

It isn't how full our church is, or how many pastoral meetings I navigated correctly that day. It's not how big of a turn out we had at our latest event or service. No, how I am known as a believer who believes is by my love for others. A big Jesus is too big for just me. I am supposed to share Him and His love with my neighbors.

A few years ago, I was thinking about the verse in Mark 12 and the neighborhood we lived in. I had a friend who had come over to help me do some yard work on the outside of my home. He could tell I was in deep thought and asked me what I was contemplating. I brought up what Jesus calls the greatest commandment and said this:

"I am just wondering why our neighborhood is different because we live in it. It's supposed to be, isn't it? If Jesus says to love our neighbors as ourselves. I am just thinking about if I've welcomed Jesus into the neighborhood and loved my neighbors?" Yard work has a way of sending you into deep thought. On this hot spring day, this was mine. I had been thinking about all that I did on a day-to-day basis to love those who I worked with and those that I pastored, but what about my neighborhood? Was our street any different because we lived in it and brought love to our neighbors, or had I turned my love off and forgotten about the greatest commandment? It was food for thought, but I knew I wanted to make a better effort at loving those that I lived by. I told my friend about what I was thinking, and we decided to pray for those that lived on my street. I wanted them to know a big Jesus and experience real love. Not love that is man-made or defined by the world. I wanted them to know about the type of love that Jesus has. The kind like in 1 Corinthians 13.

Love is large and incredibly patient. Love is gentle and consistently kind to all. It refuses to be jealous when blessing comes to someone else. Love does not brag about one's achievements nor inflate its own importance. Love does not traffic in shame and disrespect, nor selfishly seek its own honor. Love is not easily irritated or quick to take offense. Love joyfully celebrates honesty and finds no delight in what is wrong. Love is a safe place of shelter, for it never stops believing the best for others. Love never takes failure as defeat, for it never gives up. Love never stops loving.

1 Corinthians 13:4-8, TPT

This is the kind of love that Jesus is talking about in Mark 12 and John 13. This is neighborhood love. I threw up a simple prayer and invited Jesus into my neighborhood, and I asked Him to give me opportunities to show this kind of love to my neighbors. I also prayed that it would come in a way that wasn't forced or over the top, but that it would simply be *large love*. We finished what we were working on, and I didn't think much about it again… at least not until I met Ricardo.

About a week after I prayed that prayer that was like an invitation to Jesus, I was driving home from a full day at the office. Normally, on weekdays, when I get home, I'll spend a quiet evening with beautiful Sarahbeth. Maybe we'll have people over or maybe we'll do our own thing enjoying whatever hobby has our attention that day, but not on Thursdays. Thursday is date night. These days are special. Whenever I get home on Thursdays it's usually a quick workout and then after I clean up, we go out for an evening of fresh romance. This particular date night we were going to dinner and then to see a movie. As I pulled up to my home, I whipped out my iPhone and opened an app to purchase our tickets. Just as I finished the transaction, I noticed in the rearview mirror of my truck a teenage boy standing behind my vehicle right in the entrance of our driveway.

What in the world is this kid doing? I thought to myself. I could tell there was something he was intentionally looking at and there was a reason for why he was here. I opened the door, and right as I began to ask him what he needed, a little Chihuahua dog crawled out from under my truck and jumped right into my lap.

"Hey bro, is this your dog?!" I said, as I wrestled the furry intruder out of my truck.

"Yes. I am sorry. I don't know why he ran under your truck. He has never done something like this before!" The kid replied.

I walked over to the boy and handed him his dog. I noticed that I had fur all over me as I asked the kid his name. He was about five-and-a-half feet tall and sweaty. Maybe it was because he had been chasing his dog, or perhaps he had been doing yard work. Either way, you could tell how hot the day was just by looking at this kid. He had on a Black Sabbath T-shirt and wore a smile that covered his entire face.

"I am Ricardo. I live right down there! It's just a few houses down. The one with the yellow siding!" He said, as he pointed down the street. There were about four houses between his and mine and somehow his dog had gotten out of the house and made a run for it. Apparently, my truck seemed like a good place to take refuge. I quickly jumped into a conversation with Ricardo where he told me he was sixteen and that he attended a high school just a couple blocks away. The whole time he was standing in front of me, I kept thinking about my prayer. So I took the next open moment and asked him if he knew Jesus.

"Ahh I know about him. Nothing too serious though!" Ricardo said, still wearing that smile. "I mean I've been to church and all, and the youth pastor there is a friendly guy. But that's about it!" He continued.

I told him all about Jesus and how He loved him so much. I asked him if there was anything I could pray for, and he paused as he thought about it. It was like he had a lightbulb go off in his head when he looked at me and asked for prayer for his grades. So I did, and afterwards I gave him my number.

"If you want to talk more about Jesus or even if you just want to come over and hang, here is my number!" I didn't know if he would take me up on the offer or if maybe he thought I was crazy. We said goodbye and Ricardo headed home to the house with the yellow siding as he carried his dog in hand. I closed my truck door and headed into the house. When I got inside, I told beautiful Sarahbeth about the new friend I had just made, and right as I finished, I heard my phone go off. I had a text from Ricardo.

Hey Aaron. It's Ricardo. Is it still cool if I come over and hang? We could even talk a little more about Jesus.

It hadn't even been half an hour since Ricardo left our driveway. He was already taking me up on my offer. I showed my bride the text and she insisted we invite him to the movie and buy him dinner. So I extended the offer, and on the way to our date, we were picking up a sixteen-year-old boy to tag along. I pulled into the house with the yellow siding and out ran Ricardo.

"Alright Ricardo, your choice. Do you want Mexican food, burgers, or sushi?" I asked as he climbed into the car.

"Well I've never had sushi before! What if we try that?" He had made his pick. So we searched for the closest sushi restaurant to the theater and headed to dinner.

At dinner, Ricardo asked more questions about the Bible than I knew what to do with. Questions like: *What is communion and why do Christians take it?* and *Does the Bible have anything to say about aliens?* You know, the easy stuff to answer! Since he was asking crazy questions, we thought we would ask one back!

"What sushi roll do you want?" His eyes popped as he looked at the menu. If you've never ordered sushi before, it can be an overwhelming task. We ended up ordering for him, and we laughed at all his facial expressions as Ricardo tried each of the different rolls we ordered. When it was all said and done, he said he probably should've chosen the burger option. After dinner, we headed to the movies. As we walked in, I noticed Ricardo looking all around the high ceiling lobby, taking everything in. We ordered popcorn and candy so we would have the full experience. We made a stop at the butter station and then entered into theater room no. 5. We got all cozy in our seats with snacks in hand as the previews began to roll. I looked to the seat on my right and Ricardo was still wearing that extra-large smile. I leaned over to share my candy with him as I said:

"Bro, don't you love the movies? It's always so fun."

I was shocked by his reply. "I've actually never been before. This is my first time to come to a movie theater. It's amazing, I never knew it was this cool!"

He shared with me how his mom worked two jobs and that they had never made time to come. It now made sense to me why he was so intrigued by the butter machine next to the concession stand. By the end of the movie, there wasn't a single piece of popcorn left and all of our candy boxes were completely empty. The entire way home we talked about how awesome the graphics were and how the surround sound shook our seats. Ricardo shared about how he needed to use the restroom but decided to hold it to the end so he wouldn't miss any of the movie.

"Welcome to the movies buddy. We all know the feeling." I laughed. We pulled up to the house with the yellow siding, and as Ricardo was getting out of the car, we invited him back to our house anytime and welcomed him to join us for church that coming weekend. Saturday night, about 10:00 p.m., I got text from him asking if he could still tag along. I responded by telling him *of course,* and that next morning he was waiting outside his house when we pulled up. The entire service, that smile never left his face. At the end of the message, when the alter call began, guess who was the first one to give their life to Jesus? It was Ricardo.

It's crazy how a chihuahua jumping into your car can turn into a sixteen-year-old boy giving his life to Jesus. I guess that's what happens when you invite Jesus into the neighborhood. He brings with him neighborhood love. Every once in a while, I still see Ricardo walking his dog down the street. He's always wearing that smile.

Believe it or not, that wasn't the last time a neighbor would stumble upon our driveway. One time, these three middle school boys knocked on our door to ask for a drink of water. They had been riding their bikes through the streets and apparently their parents never told them not to knock on strangers' doors. I ended up building a relationship with those three boys and my house became the regular water stop. However, once they realized we were nice people, they started asking for snacks too. One of the times they stopped by, we built a homemade ramp for them to ride over with their bicycles. It was epic. The leader of the three boys, whose name was Alex, also gave his life to Jesus. For him, it happened in our front yard.

Another time we had an elderly neighbor come to our house and ring the doorbell. He knew we were Christians and he had just received a pretty serious life-threatening diagnosis. He came to ask for prayer. Today, he is completely healthy and no longer has that disease. I didn't realize how easy it could be to love your neighbor if you just took time and invited Jesus into the neighborhood. It seemed like our house just became a magnet for strangers who lived next door. The thing is, pretty quickly, they were no longer strangers.

One of the descriptions of love in 1 Corinthians 13 is that *love is a safe place of shelter.* When I think about our home on Wilshire Blvd, I ask Jesus to make it just that. We never put out flyers or had signs that offered prayer. We never even put it out through the neighborhood Facebook page. We simply sent Jesus an invitation into the neighborhood so He could help us with the second half of the greatest commandment: Love your neighbor as yourself. Not just when it's convenient but when it interrupts date night too. In verse 9 of Romans 12 it says this. (NLT)

Don't just pretend to love others. Really love them.

I don't want to turn off my love and only pretend to love my neighborhood. I want to really love them and see them come to know a big Jesus. I used to think it was difficult and just wanted to stay to ourselves whenever I got home. However, really loving your neighbors isn't as difficult as it seems when a big Jesus comes around. Truth be told, I think maybe He was the one to send that little chihuahua to our house. I think loving our neighbors is more about taking advantage of the opportunities that Jesus gives us rather than going out and making opportunities ourselves. People can always tell if you're really loving them or if you're trying to make neighborhood love happen because it's what Christians are "supposed" to do. I don't think the Samaritan man was out looking for someone to love that day he stumbled upon the wounded man who had been beaten by thieves. I think it was just that he stumbled into an opportunity to love his neighbor. Maybe the good Samaritan had just been praying to God a few days earlier, inviting Him into the community. Who knows? What we do know is, when he stumbled upon a stranger that he didn't know, he loved him. The account of this is in Luke 10. In verse 33 it says:

*But a certain Samaritan, as he journeyed, came where he was. And **when he saw him, he had compassion.** Emphasis added.*

There were two other men who previously passed the wounded one by. One was a pastor and the other a worship leader. If you don't believe me, go read the account. The first was a priest, the second a Levite. They must've had difficult meetings in the office that day and turned their love off. When the Samaritan man came by, he was filled with compassion and didn't just pretend, but he really loved him. Jesus calls him the neighbor.

> So which of these three do you think **was neighbor to him** who fell among the thieves?" And he said, "He who showed mercy on him." Emphasis added.
>
> Luke 10:36-37

The one who really loved and was filled with compassion was the one who was a neighbor to the wounded man. The greatest commandment is this: love God and love your neighbor as yourself. I think these moments to be filled with compassion for others actually come as opportunities. When they come, it's as simple as not passing your neighbor by; that's neighborhood love.

If you've ever turned your love off, it's easy to get it back on. Just ask Jesus. He helps us keep our love on and He is always quick to remind us how *love is large*. I think our neighborhoods are just waiting for us to send Jesus prayers that are like invitations for Him to come. I bet there are a lot more opportunities for us to show neighborhood love than we realize. It's not our yard signs or how green our grass is that tells the neighborhood we are disciples of Jesus. No, it's our love for them. That's how they know. I think all of our neighborhoods probably have Ricardos and Alexes in them. They probably have elderly neighbors with serious diagnoses too. I bet if you ask Jesus, He will show you just how big He is and that the greatest commandment is not that difficult, especially when He responds to that invitation and comes around with His neighborhood love.

"Thank you, Jesus, that YOU are love and that you always show up! Would you destroy any box I have around how big you can be in my neighborhood!? Jesus, would you give me the faith to live free from fear and help me to love deeply on my neighbors!?"

Chapter 12

GANG LEADERS AND
WITCH DOCTORS

Jesus is the one with the highest name!

About a week after I gave my life to Jesus at that cold, windy track meet, I went to my church's youth group and told the youth pastor about what had happened. I shared all about the events that took place and told him that I wanted to know as much about Jesus as possible. He listened to every word I said and then afterwards, he did what any good youth pastor would do, he invited me to El Salvador.

Every year, our church would take a trip in the summer to the capital city, San Salvador. There, we would stay with a local pastor and serve the church and community in any way we could. My youth pastor and his team were getting ready to take a trip in just a couple of weeks and I was the newest member to join the group. The church helped me fundraise and just a few days after my high school graduation, we were at the airport and on our way to San Salvador. The city is beautiful and lush, it has a tropical climate, and it is scorching hot all year round. The summer is known as the rainy season, so during those months, everything is extra green, and the humidity is no joke. The city itself is pinned between Lake llopango and El Boquerón, a six-thousand-foot volcano. The western side of the city is actually built on the slope of the lava mountain. It is as exotic as it sounds, and the people are just as amazing. It seems like you can't go anywhere without someone saying hello or smiles coming your way. The culture is one of top hospitality, and you're sure to be offered a homemade meal multiple times a day. I could tell you about the rice and beans and how amazing the flavor is from a Salvadorian kitchen, or maybe how the fresh squeezed juice and fruit are second to none, but the real star of the show is the pupusa! A pupusa is the national dish in El Salvador. It's a thick griddle cake that is made with rice flour and stuffed with savory fillings like beef and chicken, with cheese and beans. All fresh from the surrounding areas, of course, and everyone is eager for you to try their famous version of it. Nonetheless, as beautiful as the culture and climate of San Salvador is, it's criminal gangs that dominate life in the city. It's one of the biggest issues and it's everywhere. Most places that we went were surrounded with guards and military personnel. We were all strictly told to never go anywhere alone and not to wander away from the group. Although, a few of us did play a prank on the leaders and made them think we snuck out in the night to go get wings. I might have been saved, but I was still a teenager looking for a good laugh. We actually had the wings delivered. Our youth pastor's veins looked like they were going to pop straight out of his neck when he rebuked us. That was, until he realized it was a prank and we never left. I still give him a hard time about it to this day.

As strict as we were about safety, there was one place in particular that we went that I remember not having security. It was to the city slums. The people in this district of the city didn't have running water or electricity. They had no air conditioning to keep them cool, and the environment in which they lived was very unsanitary. The first week of our trip we would spend every evening putting on church services underneath a green aluminum roof that covered a random plot of cement in the middle of this area. Our team would do live worship, and someone would preach about how big Jesus is and how His name is the name above every other name. We would invite as many as we could to come underneath the Lordship and name of Jesus. Each night would end with us praying for anyone and everyone who needed it. The first night, we had a man come into the service that lived nearby. He had heard the music playing and came to see what was going on. The man was probably in his late fifties to early sixties and used a cane to walk because his upper body was almost completely parallel to the ground. Years prior, he had fallen out of a tree and the fall had caused his back to become dislocated. I watched as one of the leaders on our team laid his hands on the man and prayed a simple prayer similar to this:

"In the name of Jesus, back be healed and pain in the body, leave!"

He didn't shout or scream at the man. It was gentle as a touch when he said Jesus' name. I remember being in total shock as his back shot straight up and he dropped his cane. The man's eyes got big and wide, and he didn't say a word to anyone, he just took off running. About twenty minutes later, he came back, and he had his entire family with him. They all gave their lives to Jesus that night as they cried over how their grandfather was healed in Jesus' name. It was wild. I had never seen anything like it.

During the day, we would come several hours early and split into smaller teams to go around the neighborhood, inviting people to the service that would take place later that evening. To some, we would minister and pray for them right there in their home. We would tell them about the man with the dislocated back and ask if they had anything we could pray for. After we left one house, we would go to the next. Our hope was to hit as many homes as we could.

Just after lunch on the third day of this same routine, we came to a house that was white and had a gate at the front of it. The gate was shut, but we shouted out, asking if anyone was home. A sweet young El Salvadorian lady came to meet us. She seemed a little paranoid as she asked us what we wanted.

"Hi, we wanted to invite you and your family out to the aluminum patio. We're doing services in the evening where there will be live music. We will also have a short skit for the kids." The leader in our group explained to the lady. The whole time we were there, she seemed a little skeptical and worried. We told her we were Christians and believed in a really big Jesus and asked if we could pray for her. Before she could even respond, she started crying. We weren't exactly sure what was going on, so we asked her if she was okay.

"It's my mother. There is something not right with her," she said.

"What do you mean? Is she here?" We asked. The lady began to tell us how her mother had gotten involved with the local witch doctor and seemed to be oppressed. She couldn't tell us what exactly was going on, and all she knew was that her mother wasn't herself and that she had been sick. She also said it all started the day she went to see this witch doctor.

"She is here inside. Can Jesus heal her if y'all come inside to pray?" She asked us. Our group leader was quick to say yes, and the lady led us into the house. This is the point where I need to tell you that the other students and I were a little freaked out. Let me remind you that, up to this point, I had only about a month's worth of history with Jesus. I didn't know the power of His name and that it's higher than any other. I was all for prayer and inviting people to service, but this seemed a little too out there for me. Regardless, I wasn't about to stay on the street by myself, so we all went in. I'll never forget the moment I saw the mother. She was in a dark corner of the room, sitting alone. Her eyes seemed completely lifeless, and she didn't even acknowledge us as we walked in. When her daughter told her mom that we were here to pray for her, she started to hiss at us. I slid behind our group leader and timidly followed him to where the woman was sitting. He asked her if he could lay hands on her to pray and she made a noise that sounded similar to a growl. The daughter nodded her head, signaling that it was okay, and he placed his hand on her arm. It was another simple prayer.

"In the name of Jesus, be free." Instantly, I watched as the woman took a breath as if she had the wind knocked out of her. Where her eyes looked lifeless just moments before, she now had color that was being illuminated behind tears. The atmosphere immediately felt peaceful, and it seemed as if all the timidity left with whatever oppression the woman had been under. Again, at just the mention of Jesus' name, I saw a family's life restored. I don't remember the name of the witch doctor that the lady said, but I do remember that it was the name of Jesus that set her free from whatever dark thing she had gotten involved with. I couldn't fully explain what I had just seen, but hearing the woman thank our team as she reached out her arms for a hug was something that was deeper than words. We asked her if she wanted to give her life to Jesus and she said yes! That evening, their entire family came to the service. The smile that the woman had was one that reflected joy to every face it met. I still remember watching her bubbly bounce as she clapped along to the songs our team was singing. She had met a big Jesus that has a really high name, and she was no longer under the curse from the witch doctor.

The next day, it was back to the same routine that it had been the three days before. Again, we would break into teams and hit the neighborhood slums to invite whoever we saw to come to the aluminum covered patio for worship. This would be the last night we were in the area, and we had already hit the majority of houses nearby. We decided to go a little farther out than we had the previous days, and before we knew it, we had walked way farther than we had planned. We came to a house that had a stone wall surrounding it, and there was a large entryway that had several guys congregating at its opening. We approached the men and asked how they were doing. They looked at us like we didn't belong in that area as they responded.

"Can we help you?" They said to us in Spanish. The entire time we had been traveling with a translator who had been helping us communicate.

We explained why we were there and invited them all to the service. They didn't seem impressed, and one of the men waved his hand at us implying we should go away.

"I think we're being shooed!" One of team members whispered to the rest of us. However, there was lady who was with them that heard us talking about how there would also be something for the kids at the evenings service. It interested her and she asked us to explain more about what we would be doing.

"We're really just telling people about Jesus. He loves you so much. We will have skits for the kids, and anyone is welcome." We explained.

The more we talked, the more it seemed that she was letting her guard down. A few moments later, she asked us to wait as she went into the house to grab her husband. The men at the entryway became more welcoming as we talked with the woman. They even began to ask us questions about why we were sharing Jesus while the woman went inside to get her husband. She quickly returned and was accompanied by a man that was covered in tattoos from his face, down his neck, and all over his hands. He had piercings on his eyebrows and his bald head was sweating in the sun. He had a black leather vest on that his bare arms were jumping out of. The woman introduced her husband to us, and we began to tell him about Jesus and invited him to our service. He asked questions about what we would have for the kids as he told us they had little ones. Right before we started to leave, one of our team members asked to pray for the couple and shared that they felt a strong leadership presence over the two of them. As we prayed, the husband bowed his head, and you could tell the man had a reverence for what we were doing.

"I really feel like God wants the two of you to know His goodness and that He wants to take care of your family. I don't know what you guys have been going through, but I feel like He wants to invite you to come underneath His name and watch as He takes care of you!" A team member shared as we were praying. It quickly became a moment where the name of Jesus was being welcomed into an environment where just moments before we were being shooed away. The couple shared that they had been overwhelmed by the thought of how they were going to take care of their family. We asked them if they wanted to give their lives to Jesus and not only did they say yes, but the husband invited all the men that stood around to come gather together and join us in prayer. They did, and our small prayer circle tripled in size. As we prayed, you could see by the couple's faces how deeply they were being impacted. We asked how they felt, and the husband started to open up.

"This is my home, and we want to raise our kids right. We haven't always made the right decisions, but we know we want to give them a good life. Thank you for praying with us. I now know God will help us." He continued to explain more things in Spanish to our translator, and we could tell he was struck by surprise by something the man had said. They thanked us for coming by and told us they would try to bring their kids to the service. We left and headed back to our central meeting location. As we walked down the street, we could tell our translator seemed in awe. We asked him what they talked about in Spanish after we prayed.

"You guys are not going to believe who we just prayed for!" he said. "That man was the leader of the MS-13 gang in this area. Those men that were around him were all part of the gang!"

Somehow, we had just stumbled onto the turf of an active gang, and when we declared the name of Jesus, its leaders chose to come underneath His name and surrender their lives. Not only that, but we had just circled up the members of the gang that were there and led them all in prayer. All of this because we mentioned the name of a really big Jesus.

I think this is what Paul is writing about in his letter to the church in Philippi. In chapter 2, he writes about how even though Jesus was God, He came in the form of a man and died a criminal's death. He reconciled all of mankind back to himself and received the highest name.

> *Therefore God also has highly exalted Him and given Him* **the name which is above every name**, *that* **at the name** *of Jesus every knee should bow, of those in heaven, and of those on earth, and of those under the earth, and that every tongue should confess that Jesus Christ is Lord, to the glory of God the Father. Emphasis added.*
>
> Philippians 2:9-11

Our great King has the highest name! The name of Jesus is far above any other, it's higher than any witch doctor or criminal gang and its higher than any diagnoses or diseases. It's miles and miles above fear and anxiety. In fact, if you can put a name to something, then it falls under the authority of Jesus' name. There is a day on Heaven's calendar when, willing or unwilling, every knee will bow to His name and every tongue will confess that He is Lord and His name is the highest. There is no other.

Have you ever noticed how, in the middle of a chaotic moment, someone will just shout the name of Jesus? A lot of times the person isn't even born again. Nonetheless, there is just something universal about the name of Jesus that brings peace in a moment of chaos. Nobody whispers the name of Carl when they are looking for peace. Nobody shouts out the name of Craig right in that scary moment when you slam on the brakes to avoid wrecking into that car on the highway. Its Jesus' name we shout. I am sure Carl and Craig are good guys, but they don't have the highest name. David writes in Psalm 20 about the name of the Lord. We know David as a man of war who defeated Goliath. We also know him as the king of Israel who was a man after God's own heart. He had victory after victory in battle. His reign as King is still studied by leaders across the globe today. However, in verse 7, he writes what I believe was an internal belief that gave way to every success in his life.

> Some trust in chariots, and some in horses;
> But we will remember **the name of the Lord** our God.
> Emphasis added.

In that day, *chariots and horses* where the latest and greatest of technological inventions. To be equipped with a chariot pulled by a war horse was to give your army advantage in battle. Yet for David, he wasn't impressed. He knew his strength and victory was found in one place and one place only: the high name of the Lord. You even see this play out in his famous battle with the champion of the Philistines. The story is in 1 Samuel 17:45-46. When David approaches him on the battlefield, Goliath begins to mock him. David isn't timid or afraid, and right before he wins one of the most world-renowned victories ever recorded, he looks right at the giant and this is what he says:

> Then David said to the Philistine, "You come to me with a sword, with a spear, and with a javelin. **But I come to you in the name of the Lord** of hosts, the God of the armies of Israel, whom you have defied. This day the Lord will deliver you into my hand. Emphasis added.

We know David had a sling and stone, but ultimately the weapon of his choice was the high name of the Lord. It was what he trusted in and what was before him in the middle of war. Now, don't get tripped up on the paradigms of the Old and New Testaments. We know the New Testament is hidden in the old, and the Old Testament is revealed in the new. Years later, the Lord of hosts, whose name David trusted in, would be revealed as our Messiah who is Jesus. The point is simple; the name of Jesus is higher than any other. For believers who believe, it's our ultimate weapon and what gives us a bold and sure confidence for a life of the greater.

Have you ever named dropped to someone so that you could get permission to do something that you otherwise couldn't? For instance, if you have a sibling that is telling you that can't do something you might say: *Mom said I could.* By name dropping *mom*, it just trumped your sibling's word. Perhaps you got invited to an event by someone in high authority and they told you something like: *When you get there, just give them my name.* Because it is the name of that director or executive that will get you into the door. That's exactly what the name of Jesus is like on the earth, it's the global all-access, VIP status, executive member card. All of creation knows this, it's also the name that gets you into the door of Heaven; only the name of Jesus.

His name stretches far above the heavens, and it is the ultimate authority on the earth below. Acts 4:10-12 tells us that it's the only name by which we are saved.

> *Let it be known to you all, and to all the people of Israel, that by the **name of Jesus** Christ of Nazareth, whom you crucified, whom God raised from the dead, by Him this man stands here before you whole. This is the "stone which was rejected by you builders, which has become the chief cornerstone." Nor is there salvation in any other, for there is **no other name** under heaven given among men **by which we must be saved**. Emphasis added.*

It was the case then for David, and it's still the case today. It dismantles giants and heals dislocated backs. It's higher than kings and presidents, and His name is stronger than all of the earth's greatest technological inventions. He is a really big Jesus, and He has a really high name. If you've never experienced the power of the name of Jesus, then just say it out loud. Even right now. I bet you will sense peace like a river or joy like a stream. Maybe you realize it's stronger than whatever names you've recently been influenced by. It's stronger than addiction and stronger than sin. It's even strong enough to save gang leaders and break the curses of witch doctors.

"Thank you, Jesus, that YOU have the name above every other! Would you break any boxes I have around your power and authority? Your name is like a weapon for every enemy and battle in my life, so I ask for the faith to declare it boldly today! Jesus, in your name is where I'll put my trust!"

Chapter 13

1418 PRIMROSE

Jesus is praying for you right now!

I love Romans 8. It's a passage in scripture where it describes God as someone who is on our side. Did you know that God is for you? He isn't against you or hoping you fall. It's actually quite the opposite. Not only that, but in this chapter, it tells us that the same spirit that raised Christ from the dead is living in us, believers who believe! That's where the *greater* comes from. It unpacks how the spirit of God that is in us, helps us in our weaknesses. And at the same exact time, Jesus, who is alive and well, is sitting at the right hand of the Father in Heaven, praying for us and everything that we are currently going through. All this because God is on our side. It sums all this up at the end of the chapter with verse 31.

What then shall we say to these things? If God is for us, who can be against us?

I don't know about you, but there have been many times when I felt like there were many who were against me. I don't necessarily mean people when I say that. What I mean is, there have been many situations that just made it seem as if life itself was an enemy that was not on my side. I know that's exactly how I felt the day I moved into that apartment with my mom after my parents split up. Remember Adobe Creek, room number 28? That day, as I walked up those stairs carrying my box of transformers action figures, in my Spiderman T-shirt, it felt like life had aimed an arrow and its target was our family. At the top of the stairs and straight ahead was my new room. It was half the size of my last one and not nearly as cool. Down the hall was E's room. We had the whole top floor to ourselves, and by whole floor, I mean our rooms plus the shared bathroom. I would like to tell you it was awesome, but to be honest, it wasn't very special, and the carpet smelled like dust. If you've never smelled dust, go open the closet that's in that one room in the house no one ever goes in and smell the floor. I know that you know exactly which room I am talking about, too. At the bottom of the staircase was a little bitty living area with a compact kitchen. The bathroom on the main floor was under the staircase and it barely fit one person. Straight to the back of the apartment was Mom's room. We didn't go in there much. Not for any reason in particular, it was just Mom's area and, like the rest of the number 28, there wasn't much space. We went from having a large backyard with an apricot tree and a trampoline to a tiny area that was completely taken up by the air conditioning unit. There weren't any other kids that lived in the complex, and there was no designated area to play. At the house with the green roof, we had a park across the street and our backyard was the regular meeting spot for every kid in the neighborhood. This new home, though, didn't feel like much of a home at all, especially not without Dad. However, regardless of how it felt, this would be our home for the next nine months.

I don't remember a whole lot about Adobe Creek, room number 28. I don't remember what we had for dinner in the evenings, and I don't remember taking baths. I don't remember watching movies in the living room or coming home from school. I don't even remember having a single friend over. Maybe I did, but I just remember feeling like life was against us, and God wasn't for us. It's that way when you feel like your family's been broken. Especially when you're a little kid in the second grade. You don't know it at the time, but internally you feel like everything you knew just shattered. You put walls up and close off your heart. Sometimes, behind those walls are sticky notes that are agreements to new lies you now believe. In the midst of all of that, you definitely don't talk about it, not because you don't want to, but because you don't know how. Your heart seems to throw out the good memories and your mind takes account of the bad. Although, there are a few memories that I have from that apartment that are good. There was one day where my dad came and picked us up and took us to the canyons on the other side of town. We hiked all afternoon and Sparky even got to tag along. I also have memories of E coming to make sure I was nice and comfy in bed most nights before we'd go to sleep. She'd tuck me in and make sure I was doing okay before sneaking back over to her side of the hallway. There was even one birthday I had in Adobe Creek, room number 28. I remember I got a pogo stick and would practice on the concrete pathway in the front of our apartment. It was green with a black lightning bolt down the middle of it. I practiced all winter long until I could get a hundred bounces in a row without falling off. I was the Adobe Creek champ, which was pretty easy, considering I was the only boy that lived there. The only downside to that pogo stick was the staircase. It didn't seem so cool anymore after I realized I was going to have to carry it up and down from my room every day.

One day, I came outside to practice, and I gasped as a fresh snow was falling from the sky. The next morning it covered the ground like a blanket. School would get canceled due to the weather and my mom wouldn't have to go to work that day, either. So we bundled up in ski gear and went outside to play in the winter wonderland. We made snow angels and built a six-foot snowman right in the center of the complex field. My mom even got a carrot out of the fridge so he would have a real nose. After our hands got so cold that they felt like they were going to fall off, we went back to the apartment and Mom put on some fresh hot cocoa. It's the second-best memory I have from Adobe Creek. The best memory I have is from a Saturday morning.

I woke up that day to do what I did every Saturday morning, eat a bowl of Lucky Charms as I watched cartoons. The best ones came on early, but I would usually always miss them from sleeping too long. I rolled out of bed and slipped on my morning robe. I opened the door of my room and sluggishly crept down the stairs. To my surprise, my dad was in the living room. I don't remember seeing much of my dad during those days, especially at the apartment, but every time I did, it was always the best. I was excited to see him. E had already gotten up and was sitting on the couch next to him. My mom was in the kitchen and had taken it upon herself to make my breakfast for me. There would be no Lucky Charms.

"Hey, Dad!" I exclaimed as I ran to give him a hug. Of course, we instantly engaged in a wrestling session. It didn't last long until my mom brought over my plate to the couch and had me sit next to E to eat. I still remember it being in the morning on a sunny day when Dad got down on his knee in front of us. The sun shined through the blinds and into the room, bringing a sense of joy that I hadn't felt much through the past several months. As our dad began to open his mouth, tears started to fill his eyes. His voice got a little shaky as he said the words.

"Things are going to start looking a little different around here, your mother and I have purchased a house on the other side of town. We're all going to be moving back in together! I know things have been a little weird lately, but we're a family!" That was it, we would be moving out of Adobe Creek room number 28, and we would all be moving in together. The house they bought was about two blocks away from my school and eight houses down from my grandparents. It didn't just have one staircase in it, but it had two! The backyard had a half court cemented into it with a basketball hoop. There was a massive tree that was perfect for climbing, and there was still plenty of room left over for the trampoline. Not only that, but the neighborhood was filled with lots of kids. It all felt like it was a dream. The best part about it was our home would have both Mom and Dad again. The house was 1418 Primrose.

Over the coming weeks, E and I would pack up the things in our bedrooms and move them into boxes. We said goodbye to our apartment with the stairs and to the concrete slab in the back. The two of us would once again load our things into the back of that old extended cab two-tone pickup truck and leave room number 28 behind. When we pulled up to the house, we chose our rooms and moved everything in. We both got to choose the color of paint that would go on our walls, and we got to set it up however we wanted. Mom and Dad would come check it out and tell us how awesome it was. I remember everything about this house; a lot was different here. For starters, from the time we moved in until the day I left for college, we had dinner together at the table every evening at 5:30 p.m. The TV was off, and we weren't allowed to have our phones there. While we were at the table, we had to answer questions like what the favorite part of our day was, or how sports practice went. One of our parents would normally tell us a story from their day and it was almost always a home cooked meal that Mom prepared. After dinner, Dad would get out the dessert and we would eat it as he led us in a Bible study. It didn't matter how much we told him we didn't want to do it; Bible study happened every dinner.

We also left the previous churches we had been going to and went to a new one. It was called Grace Fellowship. This is the church where E would learn to lead worship and the youth pastor would invite me to El Salvador. The Pastor had been a friend of my dad in high school, although in those days he wasn't a Christian. Nevertheless, he had since had an encounter with a big Jesus and now pastored the largest thriving church in the county. Our family was the newest addition.

Not everything was perfectly put back together in our family. It's just that Jesus was showing us how big He really is and that He really is for us. Just like Romans 8. It also seemed like in the middle of our family's biggest weakness, He was helping us. That was all we needed, because if He was for us, who could ever be against us!? It was evident that in the midst of everything we were going through as a family, one thing was for sure: Jesus had been praying for us.

In Luke 22, just hours before Jesus would be betrayed and murdered, He is telling His disciples what is about to happen to Him. They are in the upper room, and of course they don't understand what He is saying. He tells them that one of them will betray Him and this leads the disciples to argue who amongst them it would be. Boys will be boys, and this conversation turns into them debating who is the greatest disciple. In the middle of this, Jesus looks at Peter and, in verses 31 and 32, tells him something nobody wants to hear.

> *And the Lord said, "Simon, Simon! Indeed, **Satan has asked for you**, that he may sift you as wheat. **But I have prayed for you**, that your faith should not fail. Emphasis added.*

What do you say when Jesus comes to you and tells you: "*Hey, Satan has asked me for you! He wants to sift you like wheat!*"

I don't know what it means to be sifted like wheat, but it sounds intense. If I am Peter, I would probably look right back at Jesus and say something like this: "*Well, you told him no, right? You remember all that 'If God is for me, who can be against me' stuff? Well doesn't that mean you tell the devil no when he asks you if he can sift me like wheat?*"

You could probably make that argument and beg Jesus to tell him no. However, that's not what Jesus does and it's not how He responds. He looks right back at Peter and says,

*"But I have **prayed for you**, that your faith should not fail."*

It must be a powerful thing when Jesus prays for us. It's essentially like He says this: *Oh, the devil is asking for you, but don't worry! Here is my strategy! I have prayed for you.* It's the prayer of Jesus that keeps Peter's faith from failing. Peter goes on to tell Jesus that he will follow Him to prison and even to death. We like to give Peter a hard time because he denies Jesus, but I think he really meant what he said to Jesus before. That's why, when they come to arrest this miracle performer that many are calling the Messiah, Peter pulls out a sword and starts cutting people's ears off. He really was ready to follow Jesus *even to death*. Obviously, we all know the story and Jesus does that thing He loves to do and extends kindness and mercy to those arresting him. Peter is left scratching his head, confused, and then the sifting from the devil comes. However, although Peter denies Jesus, ultimately He would go on to become one of the greatest leaders the church has ever seen. All because Jesus had prayed for him, that his faith would not fail. I think Jesus is still praying for us. In fact, we see this in Hebrews 7.

> By so much more **Jesus has become a surety of a better covenant**.... But He, because He continues forever, has an unchangeable priesthood. Therefore **He is also able to save to the uttermost** those who come to God through Him, **since He always lives to make intercession** for

them. For such a High Priest was fitting for us, who is holy,
harmless, undefiled, separate from sinners, and has become
higher than the heavens. Emphasis added.

Hebrews 7:22-26

Jesus lives to make intercession for us. What is intercession? That's kind of a big word that no one ever really uses in their everyday vocabulary. Well, I am glad you asked! The word, both in the original Greek and defined in English, means *to pray for someone.* It's a fancy, theological word to say Jesus lives to pray for us. It's what He did for Peter, and it's what He had been doing for my family. The prayer He loves to pray is that our faith would not fail. It's why He lives, to pray for us. The devil had come to sift our family like wheat, but the fruit of Jesus' prayer was evident all around.

I remember sitting with my family at that round dinner table at the house on 1418 Primrose when I was in high school. It was there where we learned to talk about our emotions and be honest with one another. We would put into practice scripture from our Bible studies and find reconciliation for big things, as well as small. If I talked back to Mom, then we discussed it at the dinner table. If E and I were having a hard time getting along and said mean words to one another, then we talked about it at the dinner table. If we were tardy to school or our grades weren't up to par, then we talked about it at the dinner table. We didn't always have the best approach, and a lot of times we had to apologize, but it was there that our family was being put back together. Every Sunday at church, regardless of how kind the car ride was on the way there, I would watch my parents grab hands and pray together in worship. If Jesus was praying for us, then we could join in with Him and agree with His prayers that He is able to save our family to the uttermost.

Not only does a really big Jesus live to pray for us. He always loves to reconcile every broken thing. All we have to do is bring it to Him. To reconcile means *to restore.* You see, Jesus is a fix it kind of guy. The thing is, He restores it His way and in His timing. It normally takes laying down your rights and offenses, letting Jesus be bigger than the issue, and coming to Him. Besides, it's everyone who comes to Him that He saves to the uttermost. In Colossians 1, this is what Paul is writing about. He is talking about how Jesus is everything. He is priority and He is the image of the God we cannot see with our mortal eyes. He writes this in verses 19 and 20:

> *For it pleased the Father that in Him (Jesus) all the fullness should dwell, and **by Him to reconcile all things to Himself,** by Him, whether things on earth or things in heaven, having made peace through the blood of His cross. Emphasis added.*

So get this, it was God the Father's delight and joy that the *fullness* to everything, whether in Heaven or on the Earth, would be found in Jesus. If it's a thing that hasn't come into the fullness, then it's Jesus who desires to restore it back to Himself and it's the Father who finds pleasure in that very thing. Jesus doesn't just fix things; He brings broken things back to Himself so that it can come into the fullness of all He has called it to be. For us, that broken thing was family. It was a journey, but when He prays for a thing and He is for it, no one and no thing can stop Jesus from restoring what was broken.

It was over two decades ago that we moved into 1418 Primrose. Today, my mom is an Executive Director for a nonprofit organization that helps women who are thinking about abortion get a plan for their pregnancy. My dad is recently retired and helps my mom with her nonprofit. He is also on the leadership team as an elder at the church we started attending after Adobe Creek. They are happily married and just celebrated their thirty-fourth year of being together. E and I are best friends and we're both in ministry together. We are loving God the best we can with our lives, and there is no longer a sticky note that says: *If you follow God and serve in His house, then you'll end up with a broken home.* We're in ministry because we know what happens to broken things when Jesus gets His hands on them. Our family still isn't perfect but we're the strongest we've ever been. We know, even today, Jesus is praying for us, that our faith would not fail, and I am positive that He is praying for you too. We've experienced a big Jesus and have seen Him restore our broken family into one that's whole. Actually, in some ways, He is still restoring parts of our family, but everything He has done and is doing He started it at 1418 Primrose.

"Thank you, Jesus, that you pray for me. Would you break any boxes I have around how fully you reconcile and restore? And would you give me the faith to believe that nothing is too far for you to save? I trust you, for you are my great High Priest, the one who lives to make intercession for me!"

FOURTEEN MEANS SALVATION

Jesus is the only one who can save!

This is chapter 14. The biblical meaning of the number fourteen is salvation. You even see this in Jesus' death. He would die on the fourteenth day of the first month of the Jewish calendar. This is symbolic of Jesus being the sacrifice for all mankind, and it's the fulfillment of John 3.

> *For God so loved the world that **He gave His only begotten Son**, that whoever believes in Him should not perish but have everlasting life. For God did not send His Son into the world to condemn the world, but **that the world through Him might be saved**. Emphasis added,*

This was Jesus' plan all along, Salvation! He is the only name by which we are saved. Jesus is our real-life superhero. He is the only one that is big enough to save the world and reconcile mankind back to God. Before Jesus had called anyone to follow Him, they were all in desperate need of salvation. Peter was sinking deeper and deeper into debt as his career as a fisherman was falling apart.

Matthew had lost his reputation to the Roman government and turned from his people to help bring further bondage to them as a tax collector. Lazarus was dead. Mary was a prostitute. The man from the Gadarenes was demon possessed. Yet, upon meeting Jesus, they also met salvation. This is also the case with Zacchaeus. In Luke chapter 19, Jesus' ministry is booming. The crowds are gathering to see Him perform miracles, signs, and wonders and to hear Him preach. They all want their moment with Jesus, and some are even willing to cause a scene to get His attention. Yet, Jesus cuts straight through the crowds and heads to a tax collector that was deeply bound by manipulation and greed. He tells him this:

> *When Jesus reached the spot, he looked up and said to him, "Zacchaeus, come down immediately. I must stay at your house today." So he came down at once and welcomed him gladly. All the people saw this and began to mutter, "He has gone to be the guest of a sinner." But Zacchaeus stood up and said to the Lord, "Look, Lord! Here and now I give half of my possessions to the poor, and if I have cheated anybody out of anything, I will pay back four times the amount." Jesus said to him, "**Today salvation has come to this house**, because this man, too, is a son of Abraham. **For the Son of Man came to seek and to save the lost.**" Emphasis added.*
>
> Luke 19:5-10

The Son of Man came to seek and save the lost. That day, salvation came and knocked on Zacchaeus's door. I think you can be as good at hiding as Waldo and Jesus knows exactly how to come and find you. That's the reason He came to Earth as a baby and started His ministry; *to seek and save the lost.* At the proclamation of His birth in Luke 2:11, this is what the angels would declare of Him,

> *For there is born to you this day in the city of David* **a**
> **Savior,** *who is Christ the Lord. Emphasis added.*

He didn't come to condemn you. He didn't come to tell you that you aren't a good parent, or husband, or sibling. No! He came to save! I've seen as the hardest of hearts turn to Jell-O when Jesus comes around and starts knocking on them. It's what He is after. Jesus doesn't want our sacrifices or religious performances. He doesn't care how often we attend church services or read our Bibles. He isn't even concerned with how much Bible we memorize or how many pictures with scriptures we have hanging on the walls in our homes. Those things don't move Him, our hearts do. That is what He is after, the human heart. Isn't that crazy? He doesn't want world domination or to sit on the throne in Buckingham Palace. He doesn't want His favorite flavor of ice cream or to drive a Mercedes Benz. Jesus has one desire and His eyes fixed directly on it: your heart. Don't believe me? I'll prove it to you. When David falls into sin with the whole Bathsheba scandal, He writes about in Psalm 51. Here are his words.

> *For the source of your pleasure is not in my performance*
> *or the sacrifices I might offer to you.*
> *The fountain of your pleasure is found*
> *in the sacrifice* **of my shattered heart before you.** *Emphasis added.*
>
> Psalm 51:16-17, TPT

When David comes before the Lord, he comes bringing his heart. He doesn't go and get a bull or a lamb to sacrifice to the Lord for the repentance of his sins. He doesn't level up his Bible game or religious performance to prove to God he is better than his actions. Instead, he lays on the floor and weeps, bring God his broken heart, and it moves Him. Without bringing your heart to Jesus, you just become a Pharisee. The Sanhedrin knew all of scripture. They even had the first five entire books of the Bible memorized. They fasted and prayed daily. They offered sacrifice upon sacrifice. Yet Jesus wasn't moved. He says this to them in Matthew 15:7-8.

> Hypocrites! Well did Isaiah prophesy about you, saying:
> "These people draw near to Me with their mouth,
> And honor Me with their lips,
> But their heart is far from Me."

God had their words, and He had their actions. What He desired, however, and what they would not give to Him, was their hearts. When they could have followed Him into life and life abundantly, they instead crucified Him. The only one who could save was the one they rejected and put to death. However, He did not stay in that grave, and now anyone who puts their hope in Him can know His salvation.

My hope is that you would give Jesus what He deeply desires, your whole heart! And not only that, but that you would follow Jesus all of your days. He is worthy of it, and it is the best decision you will ever make. I pray that this book would lead many to know just how big Jesus is, that He would reveal Himself and shatter every framework and box we have built of Him. He is far too big to be put in a box. He is larger than our theological words we create to explain Him. He is broader than our denominations. He is the King of the universe and the one who hung the galaxies like it were a sheet. In the midst of giving every animal their sounds, or every fruit their sweet taste, His desire is to hold your heart and whisper to you, "*Follow me!*"

I don't think Peter or Matthew or any of the other disciples knew what it meant when Jesus told them those words. It required them to leave everything behind if they were going to say yes. It wasn't easy and there were lots of trials that came along the way. Yet, they entered life and life abundantly, because they met the Man of salvation and they walked with Him. It wasn't about a destination or arriving to the best version of themselves. It was all about knowing Jesus and being known by Him. In fact, that's what Jesus Himself describes as eternal life. We have understood eternal life as a golden ticket into Heaven, that is something that starts after we cross over from this life and into the next, but that's not how Jesus describes it. He says it like this in John 17:1-3.

> *Jesus spoke these words, lifted up His eyes to heaven, and said: "Father, the hour has come. Glorify Your Son, that Your Son also may glorify You, as You have given Him authority over all flesh, **that He should give eternal life** to as many as You have given Him. **And this is eternal life, that they may know You, the only true God, and Jesus Christ whom You have sent.** Emphasis added.*

Eternal life is knowing Jesus. That means, the moment you give Jesus your heart, you've crossed over into eternal life. We could argue about if we get to take our dogs or share a multiple story house when we get to Heaven. I like to imagine I will have my own personal chef. However, no one truly knows if Sparky will be there with me on the day I enter Heaven. What we know is we will be greeted by Jesus, and He will say one of two things to us. It will either be, *Well done good and faithful servant*, or d*epart from me, I never **knew** you*. The history I have with Jesus here on earth, and all the ways I knew Him and was known by Him, are all I will take from this life to the next. Every moment I walked with Him and He walked with me. Every time I learned something about His nature and character, every story and testimony. It's knowing Him that is eternal life, and it all starts with saying *yes* to following Him. It'll be wild and full of Him. It might even lead you to places that you didn't want to go, but nothing will compare to the great joy of knowing Jesus.

These stories are my experiences of the *greater*. They are my history with Him and each story is a time that confronted and destroyed the box I had put Him in. Every time I let Him smash the box I had built, I got to know Him a little more. By the way, the pictures stacked on the cover of this book are real pictures from each chapter. Most of them were taken by beautiful Sarahbeth. Thank God for wives who always want to capture little moments. In doing so, they are unknowingly documenting kisses from Heaven.

I want to invite you into eternal life, to live a life of walking with Jesus. It is in the walking with Him that your heart is lit on fire to burn with faith. I mentioned before that it isn't about a destination or becoming the greatest version of yourself. Jesus loves you as you are right now. Messy and all. He simply wants to walk with you through your everyday.

In Luke 24, Jesus has recently risen from the dead. He meets two men who are walking down the road from Jerusalem to a town called Emmaus. They don't know that He is Jesus, but on the walk, the Bible says that Jesus explained all of scripture to them, revealing Himself. Once they arrived in the town, this is what happens:

> *Then they drew near to the village where they were going, and He indicated that **He would have gone farther**. But they constrained Him, saying, "Abide with us, for it is toward evening, and the day is far spent." And He went in to stay with them. Now it came to pass, as He sat at the table with them, that He took the bread, blessed and broke it, and gave it to them. Then their eyes were opened and **they knew Him**; and He vanished from their sight. And they said to one another, "**Did not our heart burn within us while He talked with us on the road**, and while He opened the Scriptures to us?" Emphasis added.*
>
> Luke 24:28-32

Jesus wanted to keep walking; He enjoyed their company. However, the men were tired and wanted to call it a night. So the three of them go inside to have dinner and Jesus leads them in communion. They realize who He is, and then Jesus makes like Houdini and disappears. They have this revelation right in the middle of all this: *our hearts were burning while He walked on the road and talked with us.* It was on the journey that their hearts burned, not the destination. It's the same for you and for me.

I could show you scripture after scripture about Jesus being our savior or how He is the only one that can reconcile all things. I could show passages and texts about how through His blood is the forgiveness from your sins! Yes, He is big enough to carry all your sins too. However, I would rather encourage you to get a Bible and read it for yourself. The whole thing from front to back is about how Jesus is the savior of the world. A great place to start is Matthew, Mark, Luke, and John. Those four books are known as the Gospels and they are all about Jesus' life when He walked on the earth. There isn't a better place to get to know Him!

Maybe you're asking why you need salvation. Well, let me tell you, once you have met Jesus, you realize He makes every wrong thing right and you actually begin to discover the real you, because you were made for Him! You weren't made for Hollywood or for your spouse. You weren't made to work a nine to five or to make a million dollars. Those things will never fulfill you because you were not made for them, you were made for Jesus! He fashioned you and formed you just for Himself, and after you cross over from this life to the next, you'll get to spend eternity living in the beauty of who He is. You don't have to fix yourself or try be someone you aren't so He will accept you. Jesus takes you just the way you are. You are His desire, and He loves you deeply! Why do you need salvation? Because, apart from Jesus, there is no true life. It's only found in Him.

I hope as you have read these stories that they caused your heart, like the two men who walked with the resurrected Jesus on the road to Emmaus, to burn with faith for who Jesus is! He is our savior who is really big. If you've never given your life to Him, you can do it right now. You don't need a pastor to lay hands on you or an altar call to respond to. You don't need to wait until you attend a church service or put your TV on that one channel where someone is preaching. You can simply open your mouth and pray a prayer. In fact, I want to lead you in prayer right now. I'll even give you the words in case you don't know what to say. All you'll need to do is say it from your own heart. Otherwise, if it's not from your heart, but you just recite a prayer that's given to you, it's just like the Pharisees. You can honor Him with your lips, but don't let your heart be far from Him. A messier and less put together prayer than the one you're about to read will work too, as long as it comes from your heart. It doesn't have to be mine, but because I am a pastor and love to help people, I wrote this prayer for you. As you read it, let it be a prayer you say out loud directly to Jesus! You don't need to close your eyes or fold your hands, just open your mouth and say this:

"Jesus, I know you're really big. You are a lot bigger than I've ever seen. I want to follow you. Will you come into my life and walk with me? Teach me to live a life that is led by you. I don't want religion, I want a big Jesus. My life is yours; you can have it all. And for starters, here is my heart! Amen!"

Wow, watch what He will do with that prayer! If you've never prayed a prayer like that, I bet you feel ten pounds lighter. Now, if you've been reading these pages and you have been walking with Jesus for some time, but maybe you've built a box around Him or maybe you just didn't realize He was quite so big, let me tell you, He is bigger than you know and wants out of the box. His leadership is second to none, and He knows every detail of your life. He knows each and every place you desire to experience breakthrough. I want to lead you in a prayer as well. Same rules apply as the prayer above, I'll give you the words, but you connect your own heart. Let's pray!

> *"Jesus, you have permission to get out of the boxes and manmade constructs I've put you in. Break every form of dead religion in my life and teach my heart to know what my mind does, that you are really big. You're the leader of my life, not me. You are God, and Lord of my life. I want to see you in every day and in every area of my life. Nothing is off limits to you. Be big in all of it. Amen!"*

Amen!! Now, you just let Him be big and watch what unfolds in your life! He finds lost identity and gives purpose when you have none. He is strong enough to carry every burden and worry you have. Even if you forget to turn off the pump. He is a provider and doesn't get overwhelmed when we have a need. He prepares a table for us in the presence of our enemies, no matter how many there are or how big they seem. He even has a table when there are no more reservations available. He is always for you, and everyday, all of Heaven is cheering you on, even when storms roll in. He isn't intimidated by our shortcomings, and He doesn't get angry when we get it wrong. He doesn't yell or shout mean things at us, and He can handle when we throw stones; He catches every one of them! He Heals our hearts and restores every wound! He even puts broken bones back together! Jesus isn't limited to only moving in the church, He loves to perform signs and wonders and move outside the temple too. He responds to invitations to the neighborhood and brings His large love when He comes, just ask Ricardo. He isn't afraid of gang leaders or witch doctors; His name is bigger than theirs, and any time they come face to face, His always wins. He loves to show up and touch the lives of families in the city slums. In fact, families are His specialty. Not just in the slums, but everywhere. I've seen it firsthand. He reconciles marriages and fixes broken things. It's just who He is. He smashes boxes and overwhelms us with His love. There is no one that is too far gone or too messed up for Him to seek and save. And as believers who believe, we must never forget: He is the king of the universe, and He is a really big Jesus!

"Thank you, Jesus, that YOU are really big! You are much bigger than I could ever even know. Would you break any boxes I have around who you are and what you are like? Jesus, give me the faith to live all of my days by you, through you, and for you! Jesus, you are Lord, and I ask that you would keep me from ever building boxes to put you in!"

EPILOGUE

Let me start by saying what an honor it is to have had your attention. Out of all the books on the earth, from all across the ages, you have had this one in hand. Your audience is not one that I take lightly. Actually, the fact that you are even holding my book is crazy to me. Being an author was always something I had a deep dream to be, but I never thought it would actually happen. To be honest, I was extremely hesitant to begin writing this book in the first place. Writing always seemed like a daunting task. Trust me when I say, every possible thought that could disqualify me from putting these words on paper did indeed cross my mind. But isn't that usually how it goes when you take a step of faith? Whenever God invites you into something that requires you to lean on Him, the enemy also sends an invitation. However, his is not one of faith but one of fear, and so he did with me when it came to writing this book. Specifically, there were three thoughts that I felt attempted to disqualify me from scribing these words. If you've ever taken on an endeavor that seems bigger than you, maybe you can relate.

The first was the disqualification of age. "*Am I even old enough to be writing?*" I would think to myself, most days, as I powered on my laptop and opened the software I would use to write. The second was the disqualification of status. "*Do I have enough influence, and will anybody even listen to the words I write?*" And the third was the disqualification of ability. This is a lie that keeps many people from attempting the dreams in their heart. "*What if it's not any good?*"

If I would've lingered on any one of those thoughts, then this current moment with you, reading these words, wouldn't exist. This book would still be a dream and I might be somewhere on this planet pondering the thought if one day I could actually write a book.

Thankfully, Jesus is a lot bigger than any fear that can paralyze you in your tracks. He has this overwhelming ability to pull something out of you that you didn't even know existed, while at the same time smashing all the fear that's holding you back. He has this way of turning insecure assistants into courageous men of war, just ask Joshua. He has this way of taking forgotten immigrants and turning them into queens who liberate their native people, just ask Esther. Jesus has this really profound way of taking no name sheepherders and turning them into Kings that become case studies for the ages to come, just ask David. It's always been crazy to me how Jesus can look at us and see something on the inside that we don't see in ourselves. And yet, He pulls it right out of you. Like the same way He chose fishermen who were really bad at their job to start the greatest revival that we are still living in today. He never looks at someone and thinks to Himself *"Hmm, they are just too unqualified."*

Instead, Jesus produces, through them, something they could have never produced through themselves, and if they are willing, He forms His own image in them, making us look just like Him. That very thing is something He is an expert at. He pulls something big out of someone who seems so small, and the more you read the scriptures, the more you see God do it again and again through everyone He ever used. He is just really big that way. So, when it came to writing, I said *no* to the knock of fear's disqualifications and said *yes* to leaning into Him. And I am quite honored you chose to read these words.

I am curious as to what big thing Jesus desires to pull out of you? Yes, you! Maybe it's a book like it was for me, or maybe it's to start a business. Maybe you want to release music that shapes the way the church perceives God. Perhaps Jesus is inviting you to pick up and move continents halfway across the world and love on that people group that you've always had a soft spot for in your heart. Whatever the case, the world needs the Jesus inside of you. One of the greatest ways the earth sees a big Jesus is by small people taking simple steps of faith. I once heard someone say:

> *The graveyard is the richest place on earth, because it is here that you will find all the hopes and dreams that were never fulfilled, the books that were never written, the songs that were never sung, the inventions that were never shared, the cures that were never discovered, all because someone was too afraid to take that first step.*

This struck me to my core. The things that God has placed inside of you need to come out! Take the step. Jesus is with you and for you, and let me tell you, if He is for you, then who can be against you? He is big enough to catch you, and He is so good that you can trust Him completely.

I want to leave you with one last story. The day I left my hometown to go to seminary was a bright and sunny day. I was just a few months shy of turning nineteen, and small west Texas living was all I knew. I didn't know of rush hour or interstates. I didn't even know that restaurants stayed open later than 10:00 p.m. I was unsure of what the future would hold or even what in the world I was doing with my life. Beautiful Sarahbeth wasn't in the picture and sweet little Rosie wasn't even an idea. I had one thing set in my mind, and it was enough for me. I wanted to know Jesus more than I currently did, and I wanted to give Him everything. So I loaded up the few belongings that would be going with me on this adventure, I took a deep breath, and drove off into the sunrise. Epic, right? Not really. I bet you have a similar moment. It's pretty normal for young teenagers to leave home. But here is why I am telling you this: the last thing I did before I left was tell my parents goodbye. My mom was waiting for me when I woke up with tears in her eyes and one last homemade breakfast. I kissed her on the cheek, gave her a squeeze, and headed into the living room where my dad was. He would be leaving not too long after me for work, and like most mornings, I found him reading the daily newspaper. As soon as he noticed I had entered the room he slid the day's print down into his lap, looked up at me from the chair he was sitting in, and said these words:

"Well, Aaron, it's time for you to go change the world."

I've never forgotten that moment. I left that sunny day with those words ringing in my heart and those are the exact words I want to leave with you. Wherever the leadership of Jesus may take you, I know He is a master at pulling out big things from small people. Whatever burning desire Jesus has put in your heart, we need it. That business, that book, that leadership idea, that non-profit, that song, and that sermon. Even that small desire to go meet your next-door neighbor and exercise neighborhood love. It's time for you to go change the world. He's a really big Jesus, and I know if you are willing, and say *no* to the knock of fear's disqualifications, then you just might have your mind blown at all that He is able to do in you and through you. Paul says it best in 1 Corinthians 2:9:

> *What no eye has seen,*
> *what no ear has heard,*
> *and what no human mind has conceived*
> *the things God has prepared for those who love him.*

The world needs the Jesus that's inside of you. The one who's really big. So remember, you got this! Go change the world!

—A

ACKNOWLEDGEMENTS

Beautiful Sarahbeth: You were so gracious to let me take extended times away on our back porch to pen these words. Thank you for loving me, our family and the Lord so well. I can't wait for the next several decades with you and all that is in store for us.

Michael and Lorisa: I've told you this privately, but I think it's worth saying publicly-- you two have taught an entire generation to be obsessed with Jesus. Thank you for modeling lives fully consumed with knowing HIM and HIM alone. Thank you.

Autumn: You're incredible. I know if I have you on my team, and if I've won you over, then I can't lose. Thank you for everything you've done behind the scenes and for challenging me toward the best possible version of Big Jesus!

To the content editors: Lorisa, Autumn, Reward, Ashley, Rick, Mauldin, Kara, Chris, SB--thank you for looking at this in its earliest stages. Thank you for feedback and helping me sharpen this message. Thank you for pushing me to mature and grow in excellence.

Phil and Melissa: Just thank you. From the bottom of my heart and from my whole family, thank you. Words will always fall short in attempting to communicate the impact you've made on my marriage and personal life. I love you!

Mom and Dad: Thank you for fighting when it's hard, and for modeling to Elyssa and I that Jesus is worth giving your life to Him. Thank you for allowing me to tell our story. He's been so big to us.